MARILYN

HER LIFE & LEGEND

CONTRIBUTING WRITER:
SUSAN DOLL

BEEKMAN HOUSE

Louis Weber, C.E.O.
Publications International, Ltd.
7373 North Cicero Avenue
Lincolnwood, IL 60646

Permission is never granted for commercial
purposes.

Manufactured in Yugoslavia.

8 7 6 5 4 3 2 1

ISBN: 0-517-03069-1

This edition published by Beekman House,
Distributed by Crown Publishers, Inc.,
225 Park Avenue South, New York, New York
10003.

Library of Congress Catalog Card Number:
90-61112

Contributing writer Susan Doll holds a Ph.D. from
Northwestern University in Radio, Television,
and Film. In addition to teaching film courses
at Chicago-area colleges, she is the author of
Elvis: A Tribute to His Life.

ACKNOWLEDGEMENTS
Special Thanks To:
Sylvia Barnhart
Eleanor "Bebe" Goddard
Sabin Gray
Earlene Irwin, R.N.,C., B.S.N.
Greg Schreiner—Marilyn Remembered Fan Club
Alissa Simon, Assistant Director of Programming,
    School of the Art Institute of Chicago
George Zeno

PHOTO CREDITS
AP/WORLD WIDE PHOTOS INC.
10, 39, 50, 61, 127, 139, 141, 151, 187, 190.
SYLVIA BARNHART COLLECTION
34, 35, 36, 38, 251.
BETTMAN ARCHIVES
1, 45, 56, 59, 60, 61, 69, 79, 84, 92, 94, 135, 140, 144, 148, 164, 192, 197, 212, 227, 228, 229.
CINEMA COLLECTORS
Front & Back Cover, 6, 25, 27, 28, 29, 30, 31, 32, 33, 38, 40, 42, 43, 46, 47, 48, 52, 53, 54, 55, 56,
57, 58, 64, 65, 68, 73, 74, 75, 76, 77, 78, 80, 81, 82, 83, 84, 85, 86, 87, 88, 94, 98, 99, 100, 101,
104, 105, 106, 107, 109, 110, 111, 112, 113, 114, 115, 117, 121, 122, 123, 126, 128, 130, 131,
133, 134, 138, 140, 141, 143, 146, 148, 149, 150, 152, 156, 157, 158, 161, 163, 165, 166, 167,
168, 171, 172, 174, 175, 176, 178, 179, 180, 181, 182, 184, 195, 196, 199, 200, 201, 202, 203,
204, 205, 206, 207, 208, 209, 210, 213, 215, 216, 218, 221, 222, 223, 224, 225, 226, 227, 228,
231, 232, 233.
CINEMAQUEST: 103, 108.
THE ESTATE AND FOUNDATION OF ANDY WARHOL/ARS NEW YORK
"Turquoise Marilyn" Copyright © 1990. Reprinted by permission. 249.
GLOBE PHOTOS: 85.
SABIN GRAY COLLECTION
15, 30, 52, 74, 98, 116, 126, 138, 149, 173.
SABIN GRAY COLLECTION/SAM GRIFFITH PHOTOGRAPHY
235, 248, 250.
DAVID HOGAN COLLECTION: 244, 245.
HOLLYWOOD STUDIO MAGAZINE
Hollywood Studio Magazine. Reprinted with permission © 1987. 251.
(Sylvia Barnhart Collection).
KOBAL COLLECTION
5, 7, 67, 77, 86, 119, 125, 136, 137, 144, 145, 146, 153, 154,
155, 156, 182, 183, 193, 217, 219, 220, 223, 256.
JEFF MINTZ COLLECTION: 244, 245.
MOVIE STILL ARCHIVES
41, 51, 66, 74, 77, 89, 96, 194, 195, 197.
NEUBERGER MUSEUM COLLECTION
Neuberger Museum Collection State University of New York At Purchase.
Gift of Roy R. Neuberger. 239 (Marilyn Monroe Portrait by Willem de Kooning).
MICHAEL OCHS ARCHIVES: 170.
PERSONALITY PHOTOS INC./HOWARD FRANK
21, 31, 50, 71, 129, 149, 177.
PHOTOFEST
10, 40, 47, 57, 60, 61, 75, 87, 93, 96, 97, 181, 192, 194, 197, 200, 231, 241, 242, 243, 247.
PICTORIAL PARADE
14, 91, 99, 118, 120, 127, 128, 130, 132, 147, 157, 173, 191, 194, 196, 198, 201, 211.
PLAYBOY MAGAZINE
Playboy Magazine Cover Reproduced by special permission of
Playboy Magazine: Copyright © 1953 by Playboy. 138 (George Zeno Collection).
CHRISTOPHER REES: 248.
SATURDAY EVENING POST
Reprinted from the Saturday Evening Post © 1956 The Curtis
Publishing Co. 192 (Cinema Collectors).
GREG SCHREINER COLLECTION/SAM GRIFFITH PHOTOGRAPHY: 246, 280.
TIME MAGAZINE
Copyright © 1956 Time Inc. Reprinted by permission. 184 (George Zeno Collection).
TV GUIDE
TV Guide, Reprinted with permission, News America Publications Inc.,
Radnor, Pennsylvania. 124 (George Zeno Collection).
UPI/BETTMANN NEWSPHOTOS
20, 48, 91, 114, 116, 135, 139, 142, 143, 150, 151, 159, 164, 165, 169, 170, 171, 172, 188,
189, 190, 198, 202, 205, 229, 230, 232, 234, 235, 237, 241.
GEORGE ZENO COLLECTION
9, 11, 12, 13, 16, 17, 18, 19, 20, 21, 22, 23, 24, 37, 49, 50, 51, 62, 63, 69, 78, 101, 113, 116,
117, 121, 124, 169, 193, 236, 237, 240, 252.

TABLE OF CONTENTS

INTRODUCTION
page 4

INTRODUCTION

"... everybody is always tugging at you. They'd all like sort of a chunk of you. They kind of ... take pieces out of you. I don't think they realize it, but it's like 'rrrr do this, rrrr do that ...' but you do want to stay intact—intact and on two feet."

MARILYN MONROE

The legendary Marilyn Monroe in her most familiar guise—as Movie Star.
Eternally young, effortlessly glamorous,
she captivates us with her talent and beauty,
while offering a sobering reminder of the price of fame.

For all her celebrity and fame, Marilyn Monroe remains a mystery. Despite her apparently unending role as America's premier sex symbol, a closer look at her image reveals a mass of contradictions. Often cast as the dumb blonde in her movies, Marilyn astounded the press with her clever witticisms and cool one-liners; her success as one of Hollywood's most glamorous and beautiful stars almost belies her childhood of poverty, neglect, and loneliness; the innocence and honesty behind her sexy image contradicted that image's more carnal connotations; Hollywood scoffed at her efforts to be a dramatic actress, yet leading intellectuals championed her cause and praised her talents. In an industry that thrives on clear-cut, mass-produced images, Marilyn Monroe still surprises us with her originality and her complexity.

Our continued fascination with Marilyn derives in part from the untimeliness of her death. We regret her missed opportunities, her lost potential. We fantasize that perhaps we could have helped her if only given the chance. Her apparent suicide casts a retrospective shadow over her career, giving it a structure and a clarity it lacked in Marilyn's lifetime. Hindsight allows us to see some of her inexplicable actions and temperamental behavior as indicative of her personal and professional struggles. We understand her habitual tardiness as a symptom of her insecurities, rather than as an indication of unprofessional behavior; we realize her problems with her studio stemmed from its efforts to misuse and belittle her, not from any outrageous demands on her part.

A woman of many moods and personas, Marilyn easily created a variety of public images. She could be flirtatious and coy . . .

. . . or openly seductive. Two generations of fans remain hopelessly smitten.

Nowhere is this change in perception more evident than in coverage by the press. Early on, Marilyn had courted the press, realizing that publicity could promote her career in a way her films could not. Quickly, however, the media became an uncontrollable force—always at her doorstep to record the latest development in her personal life, or the latest tragedy. In Marilyn's lifetime, they hounded her, criticized her dealings with her studio, ridiculed her aspirations, and misinterpreted her achievements. In the years since her death, the members of the press have become dutifully reverential, honoring Marilyn as a unique talent whose gifts will never be duplicated—something her fans have never doubted.

Published accounts of Marilyn Monroe's life and career vary wildly in quality, truthfulness, and intent. Much of what has been published revolves around outrageous speculation about her personal life, in a vain attempt to explain her mystery or for simple aggrandizement of the author. That brand of sensationalism—substituting innuendo for fact and titillation for insight—remains woefully inadequate.

Instead, by looking honestly at Marilyn's personal life, and by detailing her film roles and Hollywood experiences, we can understand how her screen image evolved and how it tapped into the consciousness of an era. By examining the effect of her image on her life and career, we can sympathize with her struggle to establish and maintain an identity beyond that of the sexy blonde. In the end, she succeeded; it is because Marilyn inspires our sympathy, concern, and fascination that she is elevated beyond the level of sex symbol. Beauty, desire, triumph, tragedy—Marilyn symbolizes each of these and more.

Her life, even in childhood, was marred by incomplete relationships and unfulfilled promises—a mother she never knew, foster parents who made her feel alone and unwanted, husbands who could not understand her, lovers who deserted her. Her only lasting relationship was with the public, and her most meaningful affair was with the camera. The camera revealed her unique beauty and vibrant personality. Marilyn made her mark with the camera, and as time slips away and eyewitness memories fade, these photographic and filmic images will be all that remain of her. Through these images, the public continues its relationship with Marilyn Monroe with a passion and loyalty few stars will ever experience.

Elegance, too, is a key part of Marilyn's appeal. Whichever style she chose, her rapport with the camera was remarkable.

NORMA JEANE

"I was never used to being happy, so that wasn't something I ever took for granted. You see, I was brought up differently from the average American child because the average child is brought up expecting to be happy."

MARILYN MONROE, 1954

Norma Jeane Dougherty, 1944. Just 18 years old, she had been married since 1942.
To all appearances, she was a typical (if very pretty) young wife.
But she was destined for far more than the anonymity of domestic life.

Though Marilyn Monroe's difficult journey along the path to Hollywood stardom is often traced back to her early career as a model, her connections to the movie industry go back much further. With the benefit of hindsight, it would be easy to claim that these childhood brushes with Hollywood foretold her future career in show business, but in reality, many Los Angeles natives at one time or another have found themselves connected to "the industry." Marilyn was no exception. Her mother, Gladys Baker Mortenson, worked as a film cutter at Consolidated Film Industries, a processing lab for the Hollywood studios, at the time of Marilyn's birth.

Marilyn Monroe was born Norma Jeane Mortenson on June 1, 1926, at Los Angeles General Hospital. Gladys, not oblivious to the glamour and magic of the movies, named her child after Norma Talmadge, who ranked among the most popular of screen idols during the early to mid-1920s.

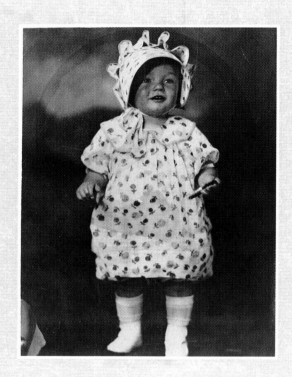

Norma Jeane Mortenson was born in Los Angeles to Gladys Baker Mortenson, an attractive woman who worked as a film cutter. But for Norma Jeane—fatherless and victimized by her mother's mental instability—the reality of childhood would be a far cry from the glamour of the movies.

	CERTIFIED COPY OF BIRTH RECORD	
REGISTRATION DISTRICT No. 1901		REGISTRAR'S NUMBER 7791
NAME OF CHILD—FIRST NAME	MIDDLE NAME	LAST NAME
NORMA	JEANE	MORTENSON
SEX FEMALE	DATE OF BIRTH—MONTH, DAY, YEAR Jun. 1, 1926	
PLACE OF BIRTH—CITY OR TOWN LOS ANGELES		PLACE OF BIRTH—COUNTY LOS ANGELES
MAIDEN NAME OF MOTHER GLADYS MONROE		COLOR OR RACE WHITE
NAME OF FATHER EDWARD MORTENSON		COLOR OR RACE WHITE
DATE RECEIVED BY LOCAL REGISTRAR Jun. 5, 1926		DATE(S) OF CORRECTION(S), IF ANY

This is to certify, that the foregoing is a true and correct copy of statements appearing on the record of birth of the above named child, as filed in this office

SIGNATURE OF CERTIFYING OFFICIAL *George M. Uhl, M.D.* — OFFICIAL TITLE Health Officer & Registrar

PLACE OF CERTIFICATION LOS ANGELES, CALIFORNIA — DATE CERTIFIED Oct. 24, 1955

STATE OF CALIFORNIA — REV. 7-1-49 FORM R85-81 — DEPARTMENT OF PUBLIC HEALTH

Edward Mortenson, named on Norma Jeane's birth certificate as her father, had separated from Gladys before Norma Jeane's conception.

Norma Jeane began life with one significant strike against her: She had no father to help raise her, to protect her, or to love her. Though her birth certificate identifies her father as "Edward Mortenson," who was Gladys's second husband, most biographers agree that Norma Jeane's father was actually C. Stanley Gifford. Gifford also worked at Consolidated Film Industries, but he abandoned Gladys after being told of the pregnancy.

*At six months, Norma Jeane struck this appealing pose for the camera.
By the end of her life,
she would have become perhaps the most-photographed woman of all time.*

When she was a little girl, Norma Jeane asked her mother about a photo hanging on the wall. The photo showed an attractive man who wore a pencil-thin moustache, much like the one Clark Gable wore for most of his career. Gladys told her daughter that the photo was of her father. Gifford was known to have resembled Gable, if only because of the moustache, and Norma Jeane fantasized for some time afterward that her father was Clark Gable. She often told her classmates that she was the daughter of the famous movie star.

Norma Jeane (who was baptized "Norma Jeane Baker") would never formally meet Gifford, the man that *she* believed to be her father. When she was a teenager, she tried to speak with him by telephone. She identified herself as "Norma Jeane, Gladys's daughter," but the party on the other end of the line simply hung up. After Norma Jeane became the sensation called Marilyn Monroe, she supposedly attempted contact with Gifford again, this time in person. More than once, she drove south from Los Angeles with a close friend in tow to a small dairy farm near Hemet, California. On each occasion, she got out of the car, which was parked some distance from the farm, and walked toward the house alone. When she returned to the car, she informed her companion that her father had refused to see her. Whether Marilyn actually spoke with Gifford on any of these occasions is not known. Perhaps she never found the nerve to actually knock on the front door; perhaps the farm did not belong to Gifford; perhaps Gifford was not her father at all.

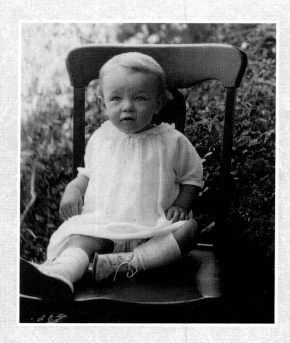

Norma Jeane's light blonde hair would darken before her adolescence.

Norma Jeane in 1928. Even in the best of times, the circumstances of her childhood were very modest.

Occasionally, the name "Edward Mortenson" crops up in early interviews and stories as the alleged father of Marilyn Monroe. Martin Edward Mortenson married Gladys Baker in 1924, but the couple had been separated long before Gladys became pregnant with Norma Jeane. Mortenson, an immigrant from Norway, was killed in a motorcycle accident in 1929.

It's difficult to overemphasize the significance behind these stories. Marilyn felt a profound loss at having never known a father. It left a scar that never healed. Her conflicting stories and fantasies about her father seem to represent her attempts to put her parentage in perspective, or to come to grips with her hazy past. Ultimately, these attempts were not enough. Just before her death in 1962, Marilyn filled out an official form in front of her secretary, who witnessed the melancholy star bitterly scribble "Unknown" on the line marked "Father."

Monroe biographers have learned that Marilyn's contradictory stories about her family point out a problem in uncovering the facts of young Norma Jeane's past. Marilyn often exaggerated, embellished, and fantasized about the dismal events of her childhood. Though a truly honest person at heart, Marilyn obviously felt the sting of her unfortunate beginnings to such a degree that it colored her interpretation of them. Consequently, Marilyn's conflicting accounts of certain incidents in her life make putting together a definitive version of her formative years quite difficult.

Two-year-old Norma Jeane enjoys a day at the beach. Her affinity for the soothing powers of the seashore would never diminish.

Gladys (left) and Norma Jeane relax with friends, 1928.

Norma Jeane's mother, who most often used the name Gladys Baker, placed the infant Norma Jeane in the care of Ida and Wayne Bolender of Hawthorne, California. Life had not been particularly kind to Gladys. She had had two children—Berniece and Hermitt Jack—by her first marriage to Jack Baker, but he had taken the children away from her and moved to Kentucky prior to her marriage to Edward Mortenson. Supposedly, Baker had left a note for Gladys that read, "I have taken the children, and you will never see them again." The absence of her first two children caused Gladys great pain, and her inability to take care of Norma Jeane added to that heartache and stress.

Gladys's family had a history of mental instability. Both of her parents, Otis and Della Monroe, finished out their lives in mental institutions, and Gladys's brother, Marion Monroe, suffered from a problem diagnosed at the time as paranoid schizophrenia. Gladys battled demons of her own and spent much of her adult life in institutions. Though Gladys was most likely manic depressive, some have labeled her paranoid schizophrenic. It was not uncommon during the 1930s and 1940s for those suffering from manic depression to be diagnosed as paranoid schizophrenic, which accounts for the discrepancies in discussions of Gladys's case history. Whatever the exact nature of Gladys's disorder, Marilyn had a morbid fear of genetic insanity throughout her life. Though manic and schizophrenic disorders have a tendency to run in families, this does not necessarily mean that Marilyn inherited an emotional disorder. It is just as likely that her early life of deprivation and insecurity accounted for her later psychiatric problems.

Ironically, perhaps, when Gladys boarded out Norma Jeane to the Bolenders 12 days after the baby's birth, it was because of financial difficulties—not mental ones. Gladys went back to work at Consolidated Film Industries, paying the Bolenders five dollars per week to look after her baby. Each Saturday, Gladys would take the trolley to Hawthorne to visit Norma Jeane, who remembered Gladys as "the lady with red hair" rather than as her mother.

Four-year-old Norma Jeane poses with a playmate, possibly Lester Bolender, the adopted son of Norma Jeane's first foster parents, Wayne and Ida Bolender.

A devoutly religious couple, Wayne and Ida Bolender lived a comfortable existence in Hawthorne, a less-than-fashionable suburb of Los Angeles. Wayne worked as a postal carrier and was fortunate enough to remain employed throughout the Depression. In his spare time, he printed religious tracts. Marilyn would later remember the couple's devotion to their religion as one that approached zealousness. She claimed that as the young Norma Jeane, she had to promise never to drink or swear, she had to attend church several times a week, and she was repeatedly told that she was going to Hell. Norma Jeane quickly learned to hide from the Bolenders if she wanted to sing, dance, or act out a fantasy life "more interesting than the one I had."

Though Norma Jeane regularly attended church with the Bolenders, she was taken by her grandmother, Della Monroe, to the Foursquare Gospel Church to be baptized by the flamboyant evangelist Aimee Semple McPherson. Della, a devout follower of Sister Aimee, had her granddaughter christened "Norma Jeane Baker." When Norma Jeane was two years old, Della suffered a complete nervous breakdown, which led to her commitment to the Metropolitan State Hospital at Norwalk in Los Angeles County. A month later, Della died of a heart attack during a seizure.

Norma Jeane (right) and another young friend, around 1930.

Around 1933, Gladys and Norma Jeane experienced a change in luck. Gladys had earned enough money to put something down on a white bungalow near the Hollywood Bowl; for the first time, Norma Jeane actually lived with her mother. At the time, Gladys was working as a film cutter at Columbia Pictures, but to make ends meet, she rented out most of the house to an English couple who had fringe jobs in the film industry. The man was a stand-in for the English actor George Arliss, while his wife was registered as an extra.

The atmosphere around the house was much looser than it had been at the Bolenders, and Norma Jeane's activities were not as restricted as before. She frequently attended the movies, most often at Grauman's Egyptian Theater but also at Grauman's Chinese Theater. There, in the famed cement forecourt, she would place her small feet in the footprints of Gloria Swanson and Clara Bow. Much later in her life, when the world knew her as Marilyn Monroe, she would literally follow in those stars' footsteps when her own prints were captured for posterity.

The reunion of Gladys and Norma Jeane was all too brief. As the months went by, Gladys became increasingly depressed until, one morning in January of 1935, she lost control. Unable to calm Gladys down, the English couple telephoned her closest friend, Grace McKee, who suggested they call an ambulance. Some accounts of this tragic episode report that Gladys came after Grace with a kitchen knife. Whatever the specific events, Norma Jeane's mother was taken away, first to Los Angeles General Hospital and then to Norwalk, where Della Monroe had died just a few years earlier. Except for very brief periods, Gladys was institutionalized for the rest of her life. As she grew older, she too became fixated on religion and the need to atone for past sins, just as Della had done.

The English couple, whose names are not known, kept Norma Jeane for the better part of a year, though they were forced to move to a small apartment when they could not keep up the payments on Gladys's bungalow. Eventually, the couple returned to England, and Norma Jeane moved in with some neighbors, the Harvey Giffens. Giffen offered to legally adopt Norma Jeane, as did one of Gladys's coworkers from Consolidated Film Industries, but Gladys refused. After the Giffens moved to Mississippi, Grace McKee was named legal guardian for the luckless little girl.

As this pleasing image attests, Norma Jeane never lacked for adequate physical care as a child. Her emotional needs, though, were not attended to as successfully.

On September 13, 1935, Grace took Norma Jeane to the Los Angeles Orphans Home Society, because she was unable to financially provide for her at that time. Norma Jeane's admittance to the orphanage represented rock bottom to a child whose short life had been nothing but a succession of low points. In a 1962 interview, Marilyn recalled her immediate reaction to the orphanage: "I began to cry, 'Please, please don't make me go inside. I'm not an orphan, my mother's not dead. I'm not an orphan—it's just that she's sick in the hospital and can't take care of me. Please don't make me live in an orphans' home.'"

Marilyn often painted a dark portrait of her two years in the orphanage, giving the impression that it was much harsher than it actually was. She claimed that she had to wash 100 cups, 100 plates, and 100 knives, forks, and spoons three times a day, seven days a week. For her efforts, she received five cents a month, four of which went into the collection plate at church. Later, officials would dispute her version of daily life at the orphanage, pointing out that the children were not regimented to certain tasks and that great pains were taken to make the children feel they were part of one, big, happy family. More than likely, Norma Jeane was never mistreated at the Orphans Home Society, but her feelings of abandonment, loneliness, and insecurity were certainly accentuated by the experience.

In the summer of 1937, Grace at last rescued Norma Jeane from the orphanage. Earlier that year, Grace had married Ervin "Doc" Goddard, who had three children from a previous marriage. The couple was trying to establish some semblance of a normal family life in Doc's little home in Van Nuys. Despite her attempts at domestic harmony, Grace decided to place her ward in a foster home. For poor Norma Jeane, it was a case of jumping out of the frying pan of the orphanage into the fire of a succession of foster homes. During the Depression, couples who took in foster children received money from the state, an arrangement that did not encourage the noblest of motivations for helping out parentless children. Norma Jeane was so miserable in the foster homes in which she was placed that she asked Grace to send her back to the orphanage. It was then that Grace and Doc decided to keep Norma Jeane themselves.

By age 12, Norma Jeane had survived a dizzying succession of foster homes and an extended period in an orphanage.

At some point in her childhood, perhaps during this hazy period of foster-home existence, or perhaps even earlier, Norma Jeane was sexually molested. In recounting the story in later interviews, Marilyn variously gave her age at the time of the incident as 6, 8, 9, or at some time in adolescence. According to Marilyn, a family friend or boarder in the foster home in which she lived at the time molested—or raped—her in his room. When she told her foster mother what had happened, the woman refused to believe her. In some versions of the story, the foster mother actually slapped Norma Jeane, shouting, "I don't believe you. Don't you dare say such things about that nice man." The resultant trauma left the terrified girl with a stutter, though in early interviews Marilyn attributed her childhood stutter to her abandonment at the orphanage.

Ana Lower (seated behind Norma Jeane in this 1939 photo) was the aunt of Norma Jeane's guardian, Grace Goddard. Norma Jeane went to live with the loving "Aunt" Ana in 1937, and stayed with her off and on for nine years. Norma Jeane's relationship with Ana was the most rewarding of her early life.

Her lack of specific recall and her overall tendency to embellish stories about her childhood have led some insensitive biographers to assume that Marilyn invented or greatly exaggerated the molestation story to gain sympathy. Those who knew her personally, however, attest to the emotional honesty in her recountings of the past. Though the details of her story may vary, the basic truth seems to be that she was sexually abused as a child, and the memory haunted her for the rest of her life.

Despite Grace's determination to keep Norma Jeane, circumstances did not permit it. Now an adolescent, Norma Jeane went to live nearby with Grace's maiden aunt, Ana Lower. The arrangement turned out to be a blessing in disguise because Aunt Ana provided the most stable home environment that the unfortunate girl had ever known. Aunt Ana belonged to the Christian Science Church, and she introduced Norma Jeane to its teachings. Norma Jeane remained a Christian Scientist for over eight years, marking her only lasting religious influence. Though the tenets of the church eventually faded in importance for Norma Jeane, Aunt Ana's guidance never did. One of Norma Jeane's most prized possessions was a book Ana had given her about Christian Science. The inscription read, "Norma dear, read this book. I do not leave you much except my love, but not even death can diminish that; nor will death ever take me far away from you."

As a junior-high school student in the late 1930s, Norma Jeane suddenly blossomed into a very pretty young woman.

Norma Jeane attended Emerson Junior High School in Westwood Village beginning in September 1939. Thirteen years old at that time, she soon grew tall and her figure developed rapidly, causing a sensation among the boys at school. For the first time in her life, Norma Jeane began to receive favorable attention. Her stutter diminished and her level of confidence soared. It was quite a change from the previous year, when the boys had called her "Norma Jeane the Human Bean" because of her rail-thin torso. Though she had fallen behind in school and had to repeat the seventh grade, she eventually made it up by skipping the latter half of the eighth grade.

Norma Jeane entered Van Nuys High School in September of 1941, but her days as a typical high-school girl were numbered. At about that time, Doc Goddard received a job promotion that required him to relocate his family to West Virginia. At some point it was determined that Norma Jeane would not make the move with the Goddards, and that 61-year-old Aunt Ana could no longer take care of her. Grace decided that a convenient solution to all involved would be Norma Jeane's marriage to a local boy, 21-year-old Jim Dougherty. The only alternative, according to Grace, would be to send Norma Jeane back to the orphanage.

The Doughertys lived in the same neighborhood as the Goddards, and young Jim sometimes drove Norma Jeane and Eleanor "Bebe" Goddard home from school. Norma Jeane harbored a crush on Jim, who had been a football star and student body president at Van Nuys High School. Jim—considered quite a catch by Grace and Aunt Ana—had a good job at Lockheed Aviation, an aircraft factory, where he worked alongside a handsome young man named Robert Mitchum. A dozen years later, Mitchum would costar in a film called *River of No Return* with Marilyn Monroe—the former Mrs. James Dougherty.

Jim Dougherty was an ambitious young man who had been a very popular student at Van Nuys High School. When the Goddards wished to move out of state, and when it was clear that Ana Lower was too old to continue to look after Norma Jeane, Grace Goddard decided that the best solution would be to find a husband for Norma Jeane. Jim Dougherty and Norma Jeane began dating in late 1941 . . .

. . . just six months after Norma Jeane (center) graduated from Emerson Junior High School in West Los Angeles.

Jim and Norma Jeane began dating casually in December of 1941, after Grace asked him to escort the budding young woman to the Christmas dance put on by Doc's company. A few months later, the courtship had progressed to several dates each week. By May of 1942, the couple were engaged. Norma Jeane dropped out of University High School in West Los Angeles, where she had transferred in February, to marry Jim. The couple wed on June 19, 1942—less than three weeks after Norma Jeane's sixteenth birthday. Aunt Ana helped the Doughertys plan the wedding, and she gave Norma Jeane a simple but elegant wedding gown. The Goddards did not attend as they had already moved to West Virginia, but Ida and Wayne Bolender came up from Hawthorne for the ceremony. Having never had a significant father figure in her life, Norma Jeane asked Aunt Ana to give her away.

Norma Jeane wed Jim Dougherty on June 19, 1942. The bride was barely 16.

The wedding was held at 8:30 in the evening at the Westwood home of Chester Howell, a friend of the Dougherty family. Norma Jeane's maid of honor was a friend from University High School; best man was Marion Dougherty, Jim's older brother.

Whether Mr. and Mrs. James Dougherty were generally happy or not depends on which account of the marriage one believes. Marilyn would later profess that she had been pushed into a loveless marriage by Grace and that she was never really happy. On the other hand, Jim Dougherty claimed that the young couple had been truly in love. In 1953, Jim stated, "Our marriage was a good marriage...it's seldom a man gets a bride like Marilyn...I wonder if she's forgotten how much in love we really were." Perhaps with the benefit of hindsight, a mature Marilyn realized how much more life had to offer outside of her relationship with Jim. Further evidence of Marilyn's discontent with the marriage includes her unwillingness to forgive Grace for maneuvering the young couple into matrimony, an act Marilyn later believed had been designed to ease Grace's conscience over moving out of state and leaving Norma Jeane behind.

In that first year, Jim and Norma Jeane Dougherty spent a great deal of time together and shared many activities. On closer inspection, though, it seems that those activities were more Jim's cup of tea than Norma Jeane's. The young couple went fishing at Sherwood Lake, skiing at Big Bear Lodge, and occasionally to the movies or dancing. Jim Dougherty's recollection of this period suggests they led a carefree and fun-loving existence, while Marilyn recalled in a 1956 interview that she made a suicide attempt, but "not a very serious one."

Below left: *Norma Jeane's half-sister, Berniece Baker Miracle, was the daughter of Gladys Baker and Gladys's first husband, Jack Baker. After Norma Jeane's marriage, Berniece visited her in Los Angeles.* **Below right:** *Mrs. James Dougherty, age 18.*

Norma Jeane greets a friend in 1944.
Her way of life in wartime Los Angeles was simple and modest.

In the fall of 1943, during the middle of World War II, Jim began to feel the pressure of being without a uniform. He joined the Merchant Marine as a physical-training instructor, and the Doughertys were shipped to Catalina Island, off the coast of southern California. Perhaps because of Jim's influence, or perhaps because of some secret ambition, Norma Jeane took weightlifting lessons from an Olympic champion while she and Jim lived on the island.

After joining the Merchant Marine, Jim was posted to Catalina Island, off the coast of Los Angeles. Norma Jeane joined him there.

The Doughertys remained secure as a couple until the following year, when Jim was shipped overseas. Norma Jeane moved in with Jim's mother and began work at the Radio Plane Company in Burbank, a defense plant owned by actor Reginald Denny. At first she inspected parachutes, but she was later promoted to another area where she sprayed the fuselages of target planes with a pungent liquid plastic. Despite the hardships of this task—the area was known as the "dope room" because of the fumes—Norma Jeane was a diligent worker who won an "E" certificate for her excellent handiwork.

Within a few months, however, Norma Jeane was recognized for something other than her work habits. Army photographer David Conover visited the plant on assignment in 1945 to shoot photographs of women working to aid the war effort. He was searching for someone to boost the morale of the boys overseas when he discovered 18-year-old Norma Jeane Dougherty, who looked quite fetching even in her company overalls. When Conover found out that Norma Jeane had a sweater in her locker, he asked her to model for his series of photographs for *Yank* magazine. Conover's appealing shots of Norma Jeane resulted in her first magazine cover and led to her career as a model.

By 1944, Norma Jeane's wholesome beauty was readily apparent.

Norma Jeane discovered that she was in her element as a photographic model. To say she was a "natural" wildly understates her ability to use the camera to enhance her beauty and to bring out her innate glamour and sensuousness. Having never felt a sense of belonging in her entire childhood, Norma Jeane now knew exactly where she belonged—in front of the camera.

*This 1945 photo by Hollywood photographer Joseph Jasgur was one
of those that confirmed Norma Jeane's affinity for the camera,
and that opened the door to a whole new world. With or without
husband Jim, Norma Jeane was determined to step through that door.*

COVER GIRL

*"Models ask me how they can be like Marilyn Monroe
and I say to them, honey, I say to them, if you can
show half the gumption, just half, that little girl showed,
you'll be a success too . . . . there'll never be another like her."*

EMMELINE SNIVELY,
HEAD OF THE BLUE BOOK MODEL AGENCY

Norma Jeane Dougherty in 1945, captured at the outset of what would become a highly successful modeling career.

*A*fter the initial *Yank* magazine photographic session with David Conover, Norma Jeane posed for him on other occasions. As his free-lance model, she was paid five dollars an hour—to Norma Jeane, a substantial amount of pocket money. Conover worked as an Army photographer for the 1st Motion Picture Unit, which operated through the auspices of the Hal Roach Studios. His commanding officer was an actor-turned-serviceman named Ronald Reagan. Conover's work, including some photos of Norma Jeane, appeared regularly in such military magazines as *Yank* and *Stars and Stripes*. Norma Jeane was enthusiastic about her new vocation, and even consented to join Conover on a picture-taking excursion through Southern California.

In the summer of 1945, Norma Jeane began her happy association with photographer André de Dienes. This image, snapped on a California highway, sums up the fresh appeal that quickly made Norma Jeane a favorite of photo editors.

Norma Jeane's ability to pose before the camera from the very beginning of her career has been widely acknowledged, though where that ability came from remains a mystery. Was she simply blessed with a natural charisma, as many biographers have assumed? Or, had she been working on her appearance because of a secret desire for a more glamorous career, as some—including Jim Dougherty—have suggested? Others have attributed her photogenic quality to her skill at attracting the gaze of men—a skill she supposedly perfected to gain the attention she was denied as a child.

For this 1946 modeling assignment, Norma Jeane wore her own wedding dress, which she
had first worn in 1942 as a 16-year-old bride. A variation of this shot
appeared on the cover of Personal Romances magazine.

Those who claim that Norma Jeane was simply fortunate to have a charismatic, natural ability regard this stage of her life as a predestined fairy tale, in which her talent would have been rewarded no matter what the odds. Those who suggest that she had been harboring a secret desire to be a model or movie star imply that she not only had some control over her life but was also actively working to fulfill her dream. And those who insist that Norma Jeane was subconsciously trying to gain the attention or affections of men paint a portrait of a woman who was frightfully insecure and easily manipulated. The truth of Norma Jeane's abilities and motivations is probably a combination of these scenarios; each of them seems to be an accurate description of her at certain points of her life.

No definitive answer can be pieced together from the recollections of David Conover, the photographer who "discovered" Marilyn Monroe. According to Conover, his reason for choosing Norma Jeane over the other girls at the Radio Plane Company was simply that "her eyes held something that touched and intrigued me." Norma Jeane's ability to magically transform herself before the camera will probably never be fully explained; perhaps it is an injustice to her to try.

Norma Jeane's affinity for animals was every bit as real as this charming de Dienes image of 1945 suggests.

Man's best friend—and woman's, too—is featured in this bucolic photo from about 1945, probably by David Conover.

A commercial photographer named Potter Hueth became interested in Norma Jeane on a professional level after Conover showed him some of his photographs. Hueth asked Norma Jeane if she would be willing to work on "spec." That is, he would shoot some photos of her and then tout them to various magazines, but Norma Jeane would not get paid unless the photos were sold. She agreed, providing she could pose in the evenings, after her shift at the defense plant.

Some of Hueth's photographs ended up on the desk of Emmeline Snively, head of the Blue Book Model Agency in Los Angeles. Snively sent Norma Jeane a brochure and expressed interest in using her if she was willing to take Blue Book's three-month modeling course. Though the agency's $100 fee almost frightened Norma Jeane away, Snively assured her that the fee could be taken out of her model's salary. Norma Jeane signed a contract with Blue Book in the summer of 1945 and landed a modeling assignment right away, though it was not in front of the camera lens. She was hired by Holga Steel for a ten-day engagement as the hostess for their booth at an industrial show at the Pan Pacific Auditorium. After the show had concluded, Norma Jeane reluctantly returned to the defense plant but continued to attend Blue Book's classes.

That wholesome look, photographed by David Conover in July 1945.

Giving little hint of the Hollywood glamour that would characterize most of her adult life, Norma Jeane seems quite at home in this rustic setting, shot by André de Dienes.

Norma Jeane's swimsuit photos became particularly popular with magazines and their readers. This one, circa 1948, leaves no doubt as to why.

In class, Snively taught Norma Jeane to lower her smile to alleviate the shadow cast by her nose. This modified way of smiling resulted in the quivering lips that would later become Marilyn Monroe's trademark. For certain modeling assignments, Snively temporarily changed Norma Jeane Dougherty's name to the more sophisticated "Jean Norman." Norma Jeane (sometimes erroneously referred to during this period as Norma Jean) was eager to excel at her new profession and worked hard to please everyone at Blue Book. She would study every photograph made of her, pick out the ones she thought were not successful, and ask the photographers what she had done incorrectly. She took their advice very seriously and never repeated what she considered to be a mistake.

One afternoon in 1946, Snively sent Norma Jeane to Frank & Joseph's Beauty Salon to have her hair done for a modeling assignment for Rayve shampoo. Frank & Joseph's had built a solid reputation by styling the hair of such Hollywood notables as Rita Hayworth, Ingrid Bergman, starlet Judy Clark, and even professional wrestler Gorgeous George. On that day in 1946, a timid Norma Jeane walked into the salon and asked if something could be done to make her look better for her shampoo shoot that evening. Tint technician Sylvia Barnhart and shop owner Frank immediately set out to straighten Norma Jeane's hair, which Barnhart has described as "brown and kinky." The strong solution used in the process also lightened her hair, giving it a reddish-blonde cast. Norma Jeane was quite pleased by the effect and wanted to go blonder. Over the next four to five months, Barnhart changed the color of the young model's hair to a golden honey-blonde by lightening and toning it a step at a time. Barnhart disputes the oft-told tale that Norma Jeane did not want to be a blonde and that she resisted any suggestion to change her hair color. To the contrary, Norma Jeane felt a lighter color helped accentuate her eyes, which Barnhart has described as "beautiful [and] luminous."

Sylvia Barnhart and Norma Jeane Dougherty became friends during this period; Barnhart often bought lunch for Norma Jeane. Though sometimes angered by Norma Jeane's penchant for lateness, Barnhart never remained angry for long. She recalls that Norma Jeane had her and Frank "wrapped around her finger." Barnhart continued to style Norma Jeane's hair for the next five to seven years, long after the shy, timid Norma Jeane had become starlet Marilyn Monroe.

More fun in the sun, about 1946. Provocative even by today's standards, a bikini swimsuit of the type Norma Jeane wears here was quite rare on the nation's beaches at the time.

Norma Jeane's hair may have been progressing nicely during this period, but her personal life was another matter. There is little doubt that her marriage to Jim Dougherty was based on a shaky emotional commitment from Norma Jeane. Still, the effect of her new profession on her marriage would not be readily apparent for a few months. In the summer of 1945, Norma Jeane was still living with her in-laws, but their disapproval at her vocation made a move back to Ana Lower's more comfortable for all concerned. Jim's mother had suggested that Norma Jeane write to Jim, who was still overseas, to ask his opinion before she embarked on her modeling career. Norma Jeane had insisted there was not time. By the time Jim came home around Christmas on his second leave, Norma Jeane had quit her job at the Radio Plane Company and was pursuing modeling full time.

Hollywood hairdresser Frank of Frank & Joseph's took this photograph of Norma Jeane in 1946, after he and Sylvia Barnhart had straightened the young model's hair. Norma Jeane had taken the first step to becoming Marilyn Monroe.

Tint technician Sylvia Barnhart continued to work with Norma Jeane's hair in the late 1940s, after the aspiring actress had taken the name Marilyn Monroe.

Though Norma Jeane seemed happy to see her husband, a number of changes were readily apparent to Jim—changes that both surprised and disappointed him. He noticed a stack of unpaid bills from local department stores lying on the table, which led to his discovery that Norma Jeane had spent most of his allotment as well as their savings on clothes and accessories. She defended her actions by telling him the clothes were necessary for her career. *Her* career became Norma Jeane's primary topic of conversation, as opposed to *their* future. She also spent a great deal of time on modeling assignments while Jim was home on leave, including an extended excursion to the Pacific Northwest with photographer André de Dienes. Dougherty's disappointment was fueled by the realization that he was no longer the center of her attention. Now he was only incidental to her life.

A grateful Marilyn signed this photo for Sylvia Barnhart in about 1948.

By 1949, the transformation that Barnhart had helped to engineer was nearly complete.

In his 1976 book *The Secret Happiness of Marilyn Monroe*, as well as in various interviews and articles, Jim Dougherty blames the breakup of his marriage on his Merchant Marine duties. He paints an idyllic portrait of his life with Norma Jeane in the period before he was shipped overseas. Dougherty implies that if he had not left Norma Jeane alone, circumstances would have been different for them. He talks of Norma Jeane Dougherty and Marilyn Monroe as though they were two different people—as if in his absence persons and forces beyond his control changed his naive, uncomplicated Norma Jeane into an ambitious, calculating career woman.

It's difficult to doubt the sincerity of Dougherty's comments. But in the end, his argument is unconvincing. Norma Jeane pursued her career with a determination that belies Dougherty's insistence that she enjoyed "peace and tranquility, security, [and] the uncomplicated joy of just being alive" while married to him. It seems unlikely that Dougherty's presence would have been sufficient to deter Norma Jeane's ambitions.

High forties glamour sums up one aspect of the young Marilyn's remarkable appeal.

When Jim shipped out again, he knew that Norma Jeane was slipping away from him. She sent him no letters once he was back out to sea, whereas before, she had written almost every day. After several weeks, he heard from her Las Vegas attorney. Norma Jeane had established residency in Nevada and filed for divorce. Jim refused to sign the papers until he came home on leave once more, and they could have a long talk. The discussion had little effect on Norma Jeane's decision. She was determined to become an actress, and, according to Dougherty, had been told her chances of a contract with a major film studio were next to impossible if she were married. Finally, in the early autumn of 1946, Dougherty reluctantly signed the divorce papers; Norma Jeane was gone from his life.

Magazine work was Norma Jeane's bread and butter in the early part of her career. She was amazingly prolific.

Earlier that year, Norma Jeane's modeling career had taken off, coinciding with the boom in exploitation magazines. Though virtually nonexistent today, these types of publications flooded the market after World War II, particularly after paper rationing ended in 1950. Several types of exploitation magazines appeared on newsstands following the war. Some were devoted to lurid crime stories, others to dimestore romance or Hollywood scandal. A significant number were aimed at men. Because Norma Jeane was not the tall, willowy type best suited for fashion modeling, she began to make her mark in pinup magazines such as *Laff*, *Peek*, *See*, *Glamorous Models*, *Cheesecake*, and *U.S. Camera*. A result of the popularity of the pinup during the war, these inexpensive magazines featured the best in cheesecake photography. Contrary to what might be assumed today, the magazines did not include photographs of nudes but displayed women in bathing suits, negligees, towels, and other scanty but tasteful attire. By modern standards, the layouts are amusing, even innocent.

The pinup magazines played an indirect role in the Hollywood star system during this era by bringing certain models to the attention of the movie studios. Although eventually superseded and later forced into extinction by the bolder *Playboy* and its many imitators, these earlier magazines provided invaluable exposure for many ambitious models who aimed for Hollywood careers.

Blue Book's most popular model wears a selection of her more notable cover appearances, 1946.

Norma Jeane posed for a number of photographers who sold their work to pinup magazines. One of the best of these photographers was André de Dienes, a fine technician gifted with a sensitive eye that enabled him to work with equal success in color and black and white. De Dienes worked with Norma Jeane from 1945 to 1949, capturing her at the peak of her modeling career. Their photographic excursion into Nevada, Oregon, the Mojave Desert, and Yosemite in the winter of 1945 resulted in the famous series of photos of a fresh-faced Norma Jeane conquering the wilds of the Pacific Northwest. Their last session together was a series of seashore photos shot at Tobey Beach in 1949, when Norma Jeane—by that time Marilyn Monroe—was in New York City to promote one of her early films. Sometime in between, de Dienes fell in love with his young model, proposing to her just before he moved back east. According to de Dienes, Norma Jeane agreed to marry him but broke off the engagement after he left Los Angeles.

Norma Jeane attends a 1946 hair show with stylist Sylvia Barnhart, who happily admires her own handiwork.

Modeling assignments took Norma Jeane to the beach quite frequently. Whether decked out in the latest swimsuit . . .

. . . or in everyday apparel, she exuded a delightful wholesomeness.

*With André de Dienes, Norma Jeane set out to conquer the California wilderness in
1945. Husband Jim Dougherty was not pleased that the excursion took
Norma Jeane away from him.*

Others who used Norma Jeane as a photographic model include calendar and magazine illustrator Earl Moran. Moran first hired her in 1946 and used her off and on until 1950. As discovered in the 1980s, some of Moran's photos of Norma Jeane, used by the artist as reference for his then-popular cheesecake illustrations, are striking semi-nudes.

Moran puts the finishing touches on a typically polished cheesecake illustration, as his favorite model maintains just the right pose.

Norma Jeane modeled many times for illustrator Earl Moran, who shot photos for his own reference. This saucy cowgirl image dates from about 1946.

Moran provided Norma Jeane with one of her few steady sources of income during those lean years when she was trying to break into the movie industry. Marilyn would later say, "Earl saved my life many a time." Moran's comments about Marilyn Monroe echo those of other photographers from throughout her career: "She knew exactly what to do, her movements, her hands, her body were just perfect. She was the sexiest. Better than anyone else. Emotionally, she did everything right. She expressed just what I wanted."

Norma Jeane's work for these photographers and her appearances in pinup magazines had a direct relationship to her later success as a movie star. Her entrance into movies was not just a lucky break, as some biographers have implied, and her modeling experience was more than just a way for her to mark time. In truth, Norma Jeane's early modeling experiences are integral parts of a long line of carefully planned events that led to her first film contract. That movie stardom was the goal of Norma Jeane and Blue Book's Emmeline Snively is evident from certain strategies and tactics employed from almost the beginning of their professional relationship.

In 1945, for example, Norma Jeane made her first appearance before a movie camera at the Blue Book Model Agency. Actually no more than an amateur screen test, the footage shows a smiling, curly-haired young model with the name "Norma Jean Dougherty" in block letters beneath her. It seems unlikely that Blue Book would have bothered with such a test if the movies had not been Norma Jeane's ultimate goal. Sylvia Barnhart, Norma Jeane's hairdresser, confirms this assumption in her unpublished memoirs about her friendship with the young model. She not only mentions that Norma Jeane discussed her ambitions with her but also notes that she was willing to endure changes in her physical appearance in order to achieve her goal.

Snively also directed Norma Jeane toward pinup modeling when she realized that the young girl's figure and natural charisma were not suited to fashion photography. Certainly, Snively knew that Norma Jeane's cover photographs on pinup magazines could attract the attention of certain movie producers.

When Norma Jeane returned from Nevada after filing her divorce papers in the summer of 1946, she discovered that Snively's plans for her had grown in proportion. Eager to attract the attention of Hollywood, Snively had planted an item in the gossip columns about Norma Jeane. At the time, Howard Hughes—millionaire industrialist, aviator, and president of RKO Pictures—was recuperating in the hospital from a serious flying accident. On July 19, 1946, the following item appeared in the gossip column of the *Los Angeles Times*: "Howard Hughes is on the mend. Picking up a magazine, he was attracted by the cover girl and promptly instructed an aide to sign her for pictures. She is Norma Jeane Dougherty, a model."

Norma Jeane did not need much time to establish herself as one of America's leading pinup models. Her ability to communicate directly to the camera—and thus to the viewer—helped ensure her success.

Over the past months, Norma Jeane had appeared on the cover of *Laff* magazine four times, using her real name as well as her alias, "Jean Norman." Hughes—notorious for his interest in pretty women—supposedly glanced at pinup magazines for the purposes of discovering starlets; it is possible that he saw her on these covers. A Hughes aide did make an inquiry about Norma Jeane, but whether Hughes himself had noticed her magazine covers remains unknown.

Always on the lookout for fresh, new faces, Hollywood executives regularly perused pinup magazines. By 1946, Norma Jeane had attracted the attention of no less a movie mogul than Howard Hughes.

Over the years, this story has been endlessly recounted and reinterpreted until the facts have become overshadowed by publicity and myth. In some versions of the story, Emmeline Snively sent the publicity notice to powerful Hollywood columnists Louella Parsons and Hedda Hopper because they owed her a favor. Snively's version of the notice read, "Howard Hughes must be on the road to recovery. He turned over in his iron lung and wanted to know more about Jean Norman, this month's cover girl on *Laff* magazine." In simpler recountings of the tale, Hughes supposedly noticed Norma Jeane because she appeared on four or five magazine covers in a single month, prompting him to track her down.

The particulars of the story aside, Hughes's nominal interest in Norma Jeane was parlayed by her new agent into grabbing the attention of other film studios, most notably Twentieth Century-Fox. Realizing the need for professional help if Norma Jeane were to snag a movie contract, Snively had enlisted the aid of agent Helen Ainsworth of the National Concert Artists Corporation. After fielding some of the calls herself, Ainsworth handed Norma Jeane over to one of the agency's talent representatives, Harry Lipton. Almost immediately, Lipton set up a meeting with Ben Lyon, the casting director at Fox.

Norma Jeane must have known that the odds were stacked against her, and that a break that might lead to movie stardom was unlikely. But this only strengthened her resolve to reach her goal. Marilyn recalled later, "I used to think as I looked out on the Hollywood night, 'There must be thousands of girls sitting alone like me, dreaming of becoming a movie star. But I'm not going to worry about them. I'm dreaming the hardest.'"

Photographer Bruno Bernard, "Bernard of Hollywood," got a Laff *cover from the same 1946 session that produced this whimsical image.*

The starfish motif continues, this time with a particularly nautical twist. Next stop on Norma Jeane's voyage: Twentieth Century-Fox.

STARLET

"I kept driving past the theater with my name on the marquee. 'Marilyn Monroe.' Was I excited. I wished they were using 'Norma Jeane' so that all the kids at the home and schools who never noticed me could see it."

MARILYN MONROE, ON THE RELEASE OF *LADIES OF THE CHORUS* IN 1948

Hollywood in the late 1940s was well stocked with ambitious,
pretty girls who hoped to make it big in the movies.
One of them was a young model who had taken the name Marilyn Monroe.
Like other starlets, Marilyn would quickly discover that the path
to full-fledged stardom was neither quick nor easy.

N orma Jeane walked into Ben Lyon's office at Twentieth Century-Fox in July of 1946 unsure of her future but certain of her goals. Lyon interviewed her about her background and inquired about any training she might have had in show business. A nervous and frightened Norma Jeane admitted that she had no training or experience, but she volunteered, "I've tried to pick up all the camera experience I can around the photographers who've used me."

New Twentieth Century-Fox contract player Marilyn Monroe roams the studio backlot. Just 20 years old, she had impressed talent director Ben Lyon with her charm and innocence.

Impressed by her appearance but suspicious of her naiveté, Lyon asked her where she was living. When Norma Jeane replied that she currently resided at the Studio Club, Lyon knew that she was probably as innocent as she sounded. The Studio Club, located in the heart of Hollywood, was a residential hotel affiliated with the YWCA that catered to young women seeking work in the film business. Norma Jeane was obviously "not playing the Hollywood game," as Lyon referred to it. That is, she was not the plaything of a Hollywood producer or mogul but was honestly trying to break into the film industry on her own. Lyon arranged a screen test for Norma Jeane and set up a tentative contract with her agent, Harry Lipton.

Ben Lyon had been in show business much of his life, first as an actor and then as a radio personality in England. Married to actress Bebe Daniels, he had teamed up with his wife for a series of film comedies in the States and then a long-running radio program in London. Lyon's most significant role as an actor was in the film *Hell's Angels*, the epic World War I aviation adventure produced by Howard Hughes in 1930. At Lyon's urgings, Hughes had replaced the Norwegian actress Greta Nissen with Jean Harlow on that film when Nissen's accent became too much of a problem. Lyon reportedly said of Norma Jeane Dougherty, "It's Jean Harlow all over again." Appointed executive talent director at Fox after the war, Lyon was adept at recognizing potential screen stars. He was less interested in the amount of acting talent that Norma Jeane possessed than in her charisma and unique charm, which he knew would be magnified on the screen. Norma Jeane had screen presence—just as Harlow had—and Lyon saw it.

Onetime actor Ben Lyon had a knack for picking potential stars. His best pick ever was Norma Jeane Dougherty, whom he renamed Marilyn Monroe.

A few days after his initial meeting with Norma Jeane, Lyon supervised her screen test, which was shot by veteran cinematographer Leon Shamroy. The test was shot in color because Lyon realized that the stark nature of black and white photography might emphasize Norma Jeane's lack of experience, while color film would surely bring out her best qualities and enhance her screen impact. Norma Jeane's "performance" consisted primarily of walking: She walked across the set, sat down, lit a cigarette, and put it out. She then walked upstage, looked out a window, sat down once more, walked downstage, and exited off-camera. Though the test was silent and lasted only a few minutes, Shamroy, too, noticed Norma Jeane's resemblance to Jean Harlow. Shamroy later said, "This girl had something I hadn't seen since silent pictures. She had a kind of fantastic beauty like Gloria Swanson . . . she got sex on a piece of film like Jean Harlow. . . . She was showing us she could sell emotions in pictures." The Harlow comparison would surface again in the years to come.

Marilyn's 1946 contract with Twentieth Century-Fox brought her a modest salary of $75 a week—typical for young unknowns at the time.

A week later, Darryl Zanuck, who was head of production at Fox, saw the screen test and approved Norma Jeane's contract. She was to receive $75 per week for six months, at which time she would be reviewed and possibly signed for another six months. Norma Jeane Dougherty signed her first movie contract in August of 1946.

Marilyn logged many hours posing for publicity photos, often clad in a swimsuit . . .

. . . but sometimes in everyday attire. A December 1946 studio biography described Marilyn as an ex-babysitter.

Only 20 years old at the time, Norma Jeane had to ask Grace McKee Goddard to cosign the contract for her. Though Grace readily obliged, there were really very few family members to rejoice in Norma Jeane's first success. Grace and Doc Goddard had moved back to California after the war, but the relationship between Grace and Norma Jeane remained strained. Norma Jeane's mother, Gladys Baker, had been released from a San Francisco institution in 1945, just as her daughter's modeling career was getting underway, but Gladys had been unable to withstand the pressures of everyday life. She had returned to an institution, this time in Los Angeles, by the time Norma Jeane signed that first contract. Because Norma Jeane and Jim Dougherty were on the verge of divorce, she had lost contact with the Dougherty clan as well. The aging Ana Lower remained her only close family tie.

Norma Jeane chose to celebrate her good fortune with her new associates—Ben Lyon and Bebe Daniels. The first order of business was to change the young actress's name—Lyon utterly loathed "Norma Jeane Dougherty." Lyon remembered a stage actress from the 1920s whom he had long admired—a musical performer named Marilyn Miller. He thought "Marilyn" would better suit Norma Jeane's new, glamorous identity as a Hollywood starlet. For her part, Norma Jeane suggested her mother's family name, "Monroe," as a last name. Lyon liked the alliteration of "Marilyn Monroe," and told Norma Jeane that the double "M" was a lucky omen. So it was that in the course of one afternoon, Norma Jeane Mortenson Baker Dougherty was transformed into Marilyn Monroe. She was forever grateful to Lyon for his support and his help. A few years later, when Marilyn Monroe was on top, she sent Lyon a photograph inscribed: "You found me, named me and believed in me when no one else did. My love and thanks forever."

Armed with a new name, and perhaps a new sense of purpose, Marilyn prepared herself for a career in motion pictures. Unfortunately, even moderate success would elude the hopeful starlet for several years.

For the first few months on the Fox lot, Marilyn landed no speaking roles in any films. Instead, she was placed in dancing, singing, and pantomime classes alongside other new contract players. She also posed for an endless series of publicity shots. With her talent for posing in front of the still camera, Marilyn brought an excitement and sparkle to her photos simply not found in the publicity shots of most other starlets. The Fox publicity department also manufactured a studio biography for their latest contract player, one that insisted that Marilyn had been discovered when she turned up as a babysitter for a Fox talent scout.

Swimming pool plus pretty starlet equals a photo opportunity.
Note Marilyn's ankle bracelet, a provocative accessory
that she brought to numerous photo sessions in the late 1940s and early '50s.

Marilyn also made a point of getting to know on a first-name basis some of the reporters permanently based at the studio. Courting the press was a tactic she would use for most of her career, but in the early years she went out of her way to do them favors. She went so far as to pose at the beach one chilly November in a skimpy bathing suit. Reporters considered her a good sport and a good story, and in 1948 she was awarded the title "Miss Press Club." One of the reporters who would remain a close friend until her death was *New York Post* writer Sidney Skolsky. Skolsky wrote an entertainment column that could literally make or break a performer's career. The powerful columnist was more impressed by Marilyn's ambition than by her lack of experience: "It was clear that Marilyn was prepared to work hard to improve herself," Skolsky recalled later. "She wanted to be an actress and a movie star. I knew nothing would stop her. The drive and determination and need inside Marilyn could not be halted."

In addition to her weekly classes at the studio, Marilyn was pressed into service as an extra on a variety of films. Though no exact list of these movies exists, some film buffs claim to have spotted her in the musical comedies *The Shocking Miss Pilgrim* and *You Were Meant for Me*, as well as in the western *Green Grass of Wyoming*. Appearing as an extra not only allowed contract players an opportunity to understand the process of making a movie but accustomed them to the unique "hurry up and wait" pace of filmmaking. Often actors were rushed into makeup and costume, only to stand around for hours until the director was ready for their scene.

Sometimes, variations on the reliable swimsuit theme got pretty silly. This shot was taken in February 1947.

Sillier still is this little gem, which casts Marilyn as an Indian maiden who always keeps her cool.

Many of the poses Marilyn did for illustrator Earl Moran found their way onto calendars.

In the spring of 1947, Marilyn was finally given her first speaking role—a bit part in a musical comedy called *Scudda Hoo! Scudda Hay!* A bit role differs from extra work in that the actor gets at least one line as well as an acknowledgement of the appearance by the studio. Graduating from extra work to bit parts can be an important step in an actor's career—many an aspiring star has been noticed by milking a bit into a memorable screen debut. Marilyn's big scene featured her character, Betty, dressed in a pinafore and walking down the steps of a small-town church. Betty passes the main character, played by June Haver, and says, "Hi, Rad," to which Haver replies, "Hi, Betty."

Marilyn and fellow starlet Colleen Townsend greet Robert Karnes in Scudda Hoo! Scudda Hay! *In the film's final cut, the rowboat appears only in a long shot.*

On the set of Marilyn's first film, Scudda Hoo! Scudda Hay!

Hardly earth-shattering material, but Marilyn was supposed to get at least one close-up. After she became a star, the Twentieth Century-Fox publicity department circulated the story that her only line in this film had ended up on the cutting room floor. Marilyn herself repeated the anecdote in 1955, on Edward R. Murrow's television interview program, *Person to Person*. However, according to film historian and noted Monroe buff James Haspiel, the story is not true. Haspiel maintains that Marilyn's brief line remains intact in complete versions of the now-obscure *Scudda Hoo! Scudda Hay!*, as does a shot of Marilyn and another starlet paddling a canoe. Neither shot appears in close-up, however, indicating that Marilyn's close-ups had been edited from the film. Marilyn's part in this mediocre B-film—remembered now only because of her appearance—did little for her career, and it was several months before she got another bit role.

One day while walking across the Fox lot, Marilyn recognized an older man in a limousine as one of the studio executives. She smiled as he passed by, causing him to stop and chat with her. The man was Hollywood pioneer Joseph Schenck, then nearly 70 years old and an executive producer at Fox. Schenck, who began in the film industry about 1912, founded 20th Century in 1933 and became chairman two years later when his company merged with Fox Films. A stint in jail on charges involving union payoffs forced him to resign his position in 1941, but Schenck came back as an executive producer a short time later. He took an immediate liking to Marilyn that afternoon and invited her to his home for a dinner party the following week.

Marilyn explores the inner workings of Twentieth Century-Fox, circa 1947.

The unknown starlet became a regular at Schenck's small, intimate dinner parties, and the two grew quite close. Allegations that Marilyn was his mistress and used that position to further her career remain unverifiable, even dubious. Given Schenck's advanced age and the fact that Marilyn's career floundered for several more years after their meeting, it is unlikely that the relationship was more than that of a grand old man of Hollywood advising a beautiful protégée in the ways of "the business." Marilyn was not the only starlet who attended his dinner parties, and her presence at such functions was probably calculated by Schenck to impress and innocently amuse his colleagues.

This 1947 publicity photo gave the nation's newspaper editors three young starlets for the price of one. Marilyn is the clear standout.

The juvenile-delinquent drama Dangerous Years
had a bit part for Marilyn, who played a waitress.

Schenck remained Marilyn's friend and sometimes mentor for several years, until she made a conscious effort to remove herself from the Hollywood scene during the mid-1950s. Schenck died in 1961, just a year earlier than Marilyn. Confined to bed near the end of his life, the elderly mogul was delighted when Marilyn came to visit him for what would be the last time. On the way home, according to Marilyn's friend and publicist Rupert Allan, she cried openly. Marilyn's respect for Schenck's power and position went beyond the level of what he could do for her career. She talked of sitting at his feet for hours and listening to his stories about Hollywood. "He was full of wisdom like some great explorer," she recalled. "I also liked to look at his face. It was as much the face of a town as of a man. The whole history of Hollywood was in it."

In August of 1947, Marilyn was assigned a role in the drama *Dangerous Years*, a film exploiting America's rising concern over postwar juvenile delinquency. Her role as a waitress in a local teen hangout was small but slightly more substantial than her part in *Scudda Hoo! Scudda Hay!* This time she was given a close-up, which is important in establishing or reinforcing an actor's image. She received fourteenth billing in a film that credited 15 actors. Though *Dangerous Years* would seem to have been a logical step in Marilyn's fledgling career, Fox did not renew her contract when it expired a few days after her shots had been completed.

And she takes dictation, too! Marilyn impersonates Hollywood's idea of a secretary in this silly but good-humored shot from 1947.

Bruno Bernard took this vibrant portrait in about 1947.
Despite Marilyn's obvious charms, and the fact that Fox had hardly given her
a proper chance to prove herself, the studio dropped her option in the summer of 1947.

This would not be the last time that Marilyn got caught up in the turnover of contract players at option time. Though the reasons behind Fox's decision to drop her option are not known, the studio exhibited little interest in developing her acting career at this juncture. Fox had seemed content simply to feature her in dozens of cheesecake publicity photos or to shuttle her around to publicity events, such as the Fox Studio Club golf tournament. Marilyn proved adept at publicity functions, particularly if there were photos involved, but she seriously desired to be an actress.

The major star at Fox during this era was another blonde actress, Betty Grable, whose popularity had soared during World War II because of her famous pinup photos. Marilyn, too, had an extensive background in modeling for pinups, but Grable also had a great deal of experience in show business. By the time she was Marilyn's age, Grable had already toured in vaudeville, appeared on the stage, and performed on radio, giving her a confidence and style that Marilyn lacked. Marilyn's lack of show-business experience may have prevented the studio from grooming her to follow in Grable's footsteps—a role the studio did assign to singer-dancer June Haver.

Out of work and out of luck, Marilyn responded to a general casting call advertised in the *Los Angeles Times* for a play at the Bliss-Hayden Miniature Theatre in Beverly Hills. Marilyn landed the second lead in the play, a lighthearted spoof of Hollywood entitled *Glamour Preferred*. The Bliss-Hayden, which no longer exists, had been established in the 1930s by stage performers Harry Hayden and Lela Bliss. The theater was best known as a showcase for the talents of young movie hopefuls, who needed to catch the attention of important agents or studio talent scouts. Students or performers from the Bliss-Hayden who went on to careers in the movies included Veronica Lake, Doris Day, Debbie Reynolds, Craig Stevens, and Jon Hall. Los Angeles theatergoers who regularly attended the Bliss-Hayden in the fall of 1947 through the summer of 1948 were fortunate enough to witness a young Marilyn Monroe perform in her only extensive attempt at public stagework.

Though *Glamour Preferred* ran for just three weeks in October and November of 1947, Marilyn appeared in at least one other play at the small theater. According to Don Hayden—son of Harry Hayden and Lela Bliss—Marilyn costarred in a production of *Stage Door* in the late summer of 1948. In a 1975 interview, Lela Bliss recalled Marilyn's experiences at the Bliss-Hayden: "She could have played anything. We never had any struggle about parts with her—she was always happy to play what you cast her in."

This startlingly brief costume was enthusiastically received by photo editors. Shots from this Bernard session appeared in magazines for years.

Glamour portraits were a vital tool that helped Marilyn find acting jobs after being let go by Fox.

While still under contract to Fox, Marilyn had begun taking acting lessons at the Actors Lab, a practice she continued after she was dropped by the studio. She paid for her lessons with occasional modeling jobs, though the Lab allowed her some leeway in paying her bill. The Actors Lab, operated by Roman Bohnen, J. Edward Bromberg, and Morris Carnovsky, was considered a West Coast offshoot of the Group Theatre of New York. By most accounts, Marilyn was a quiet and shy student while at the Lab; any influence that her two years of studies there may have had on her acting ability was probably slight.

Like the Group Theatre, the Lab was left of center in its political orientation, and some have suggested that Lab members may have influenced Marilyn's thinking. Never an overtly political person, Marilyn nonetheless always considered herself a part of the working class and remained unfazed by the Lab's leftist politics.

In the early 1950s, after Marilyn had left the Actors Lab, Carnovsky and his wife were labeled Communists by the House Un-American Activities Committee (HUAC), an official committee of the U.S. House of Representatives assigned to investigate allegedly un-American organizations, particularly those suspected of Communist affiliations. HUAC would descend on Hollywood with a vengeance in the early 1950s. The result was extensive blacklists of actors and other industry personnel suspected of Communist leanings; a fear gripped Hollywood in which no actor or actress wanted to be remotely associated with leftist groups. At that time, a studio executive visiting the set of *All About Eve* noticed Marilyn reading *The Autobiography of Lincoln Steffens*. Steffens was a famous journalist who had made his name by exposing the corrupt practices of government and business. The executive considered it "dangerous to be reading such radical books in public," but Marilyn continued to read the book anyway.

In the end, Marilyn suffered no consequences as the result of her association with the Actors Lab, probably because her burgeoning image as a sex symbol completely overshadowed any other aspects of her personality. Throughout her life, and to no detriment to her career, she would foster friendships with intellectuals associated with the political left.

Poolside, about 1947.

Marilyn in 1948. Already serious about improving as an actress, she had begun taking lessons at the Actors Lab.

Marilyn's developing talent was cultivated not just by her classes at the Actors Lab, but by a number of individuals with connections to the industry. At a publicity function in the fall of 1947, she met actor John Carroll and his wife, Lucille Ryman, a talent scout at Metro-Goldwyn-Mayer. Marilyn signed a personal contract with the Carrolls in December of 1947, much to the chagrin of her agent. In addition to helping her finance her acting classes, John Carroll gave her singing instructions. Her ties to the Carrolls were so close that at one point she moved in with them, an arrangement that did not last for long. Eventually, Marilyn moved back to the Studio Club, where former residents remember her lifting weights and jogging every morning to keep her figure.

In March of 1948, Marilyn signed a six-month contract with Columbia Pictures. Exactly how Marilyn landed her contract at Columbia is open to debate, though the consensus is that Joe Schenck interceded on her behalf. Schenck supposedly talked directly to Columbia head Harry Cohn about Marilyn's contract, though there is no written memorandum or personal testimony by Marilyn to confirm this. An alternative account is that executives at Columbia had been checking around Hollywood about her, perhaps at the urgings of her agent, or even the Carrolls.

Actor John Carroll entered films in 1935 and was built up by RKO and, later, MGM as a second-string Clark Gable. Marilyn signed a personal contract with Carroll and his wife in late 1947. Some sources claim that Carroll and Marilyn were lovers, but years later the handsome actor remarked, "The only thing I ever did with Marilyn was to try to teach her how to sing."

Marilyn signed a contract with Columbia Pictures in the spring of 1948.

As soon as Marilyn signed her contract, she went to a Hollywood bookstore to open a charge account. Her roommate at the Studio Club remembers her purchasing a classic study of bone structure entitled *De Humani Corporis Fabrica* by Andreas Vesalius, as well as notable works of literature. Even at this early juncture, Marilyn took great pains to educate herself, a practice her detractors claim was merely part of her publicity campaign. The facts show her pursuit of knowledge and culture to be sincere, however, as her early bookstore charge accounts and library cards help substantiate.

Marilyn's last tie to her life as Norma Jeane was broken shortly after she received her Columbia contract. Ana Lower died on March 14, 1948, long before Marilyn achieved stardom. Marilyn's relationship with Aunt Ana proved to be one of the longest and most satisfying of the actress's short life. After Aunt Ana's death, Marilyn told Studio Club roommate Clarice Evans: "There's only one person in the world that I've ever really loved. That was Aunt Ana . . . Aunt Ana was sure—surer than I am now—that I was right in my ambition to be an actress and that I'd be a success. But she'll never know whether she was right or wrong."

Marilyn's first film for Columbia proved to be her only film for that studio. She received second billing in *Ladies of the Chorus*, a low-budget musical featuring Marilyn as a burlesque star who falls in love with the son of a socially prominent family. In keeping with the magic of the movies, Marilyn was cast as star Adele Jergens's daughter, though Jergens was only nine years older than Marilyn! The script called for Marilyn to sing two songs in the film, a ballad entitled "Anyone Can Tell I Love You," and the enticing "Every Baby Needs a Da-Da-Daddy." For the first time in her screen career, she revealed a pleasant, competent singing voice. Marilyn's part was considerably larger than those she had been assigned at Fox; on screen, she held her own against the considerably more experienced Jergens. Columbia executives hedged their bets by setting their new starlet up with singing and acting lessons.

Fred Karger, the musical director of *Ladies of the Chorus*, coached Marilyn to prepare her for her two production numbers. A man dedicated to his craft, Karger improved Marilyn's vocal and musical skills immensely. During the course of their professional relationship, Marilyn began dating Karger, and the two became quite close. He brought her home to meet his family, which included his daughter by a previous marriage, his sister and her children, and his mother. Marilyn, who had felt alone since the death of Ana Lower, embraced Karger's family wholeheartedly, particularly his mother, Anne.

Thrust once again into the grind of publicity photos, Marilyn remained hopeful about her prospects with a new studio.

*Columbia made a smart move when it awarded Marilyn the second lead
in* Ladies of the Chorus, *a minor but pleasant backstage musical.
For the first time in her film career,
Marilyn had the opportunity to show her talent as a singer.*

Mrs. Anne Karger, whom everyone called "Nana," was the widow of one of the founders of MGM. She had been a part of the grandeur of Hollywood in the 1920s, when she used to hold open house in a permanent suite at the Hollywood Hotel. There, such Hollywood luminaries as Rudolph Valentino, Jack Pickford, and Nazimova would gather for food and drink. Nana Karger enjoyed the company of Marilyn Monroe, an up-and-coming actress of the new generation of Hollywood, and advised the young starlet in a motherly fashion. Marilyn's friendship with Nana would outlast her relationship with Fred, who never seemed to take the romance as seriously as she did. Marilyn hoped to marry into the Karger family, but when it was apparent that Fred had no inclination in that direction, she stopped seeing him. Though heartbroken for several years over her lost love, Marilyn benefited not only from Karger's professional help in terms of her vocal skills but also from his advice on other matters. He suggested, for instance, that Marilyn visit an orthodontist to have her slightly protruding front teeth fixed, a minor adjustment that improved her already striking good looks.

Within a year of his breakup with Marilyn, Karger married actress Jane Wyman. Karger and Wyman would eventually divorce, and then remarry and divorce again. Years later, after Marilyn's death, Karger called his first wife, Patti, in a desperately nervous state, telling her that Marilyn had appeared to him in a dream. He died on August 5, 1979—the anniversary of Marilyn's death.

Marilyn in Ladies of the Chorus, *with actress Nana Bryant.*

Marilyn's costar Rand Brooks had had a featured role as Scarlett O'Hara's first husband in Gone With the Wind, *but worked mainly in B-movies. His bland good looks were no match for Marilyn's on-screen charisma.*

Marilyn had a nice on-screen rapport with top-billed Adele Jergens, who is best remembered for her frequent portrayals of worldly glamour girls and gun molls.

STARLET | 61

While Fred Karger assisted Marilyn with her singing, Columbia's head drama coach, Natasha Lytess, was asked to help develop her acting skills. Lytess had been a member of a well-respected acting ensemble headed by famed theatrical director Max Reinhardt, and she had parlayed her experience into a job at Columbia Pictures. A serious woman with a strict and demanding personality, Lytess became the first to recognize that Marilyn did possess true acting talent. The experienced coach was also impressed by the starlet's determination to improve, and by her willingness to work hard no matter how grueling the schedule. Natasha Lytess served as Marilyn's personal acting teacher for seven years, even quitting her job at Columbia in 1950 to coach her most famous pupil on an exclusive basis.

Karger and Lytess's work paid off, because Marilyn received her first review notices with her performance in *Ladies of the Chorus*. Though a modest B-film shot in just 11 days, *Ladies* was by no means a failure. A review in the *Motion Picture Herald* reads, "One of the brightest spots is Miss Monroe's singing. She is pretty, and with her pleasing voice and style, shows promise." In 1952, when Marilyn was beginning to make a name for herself, Columbia lifted her performance of "Every Baby Needs a Da-Da-Daddy" from *Ladies of the Chorus* and spliced it into a war film entitled *Okinawa*.

Aside from *Ladies of the Chorus*, and her relationships with Fred Karger and Natasha Lytess, Marilyn's months at Columbia proved less than fruitful. The only other "appearance" Marilyn made in a Columbia production occurred when her photograph was used in the 1949 Gene Autry film *Riders of the Whistling Pines*.

Columbia's head drama coach, Natasha Lytess, was a major influence during the formative years of Marilyn's career. In time, Lytess worked with Marilyn exclusively.

Partial credit for Marilyn's successful singing in Ladies of the Chorus *must go to musical director Fred Karger, seen here with his second wife, actress Jane Wyman. Marilyn was in love with Karger and wanted to marry him.*

Although Marilyn (center) won some positive reviews for her work in Ladies of the Chorus, *the film was to be her only starring vehicle at Columbia.*

Columbia was ruled by Harry Cohn, the most ruthless and headstrong of the legendary movie moguls who once ran Hollywood with an iron hand. Most of the moguls made occasional miscalculations regarding an actor's potential, but Cohn was prone to more than his share because of his volatile temper and vengeful personality. According to Hollywood writer Garson Kanin in the book *Tracy and Hepburn*, Marilyn tested for the role of Billie Dawn in the classic *Born Yesterday*, but Cohn could not be bothered to walk the few feet from his desk to the screening room to watch the results. Consequently, Marilyn was not even considered for the part.

When Marilyn's contract expired in September of 1948, her option was not renewed. According to former Columbia employees, Cohn complained that Marilyn not only looked too heavy in *Ladies of the Chorus* but she also had no acting talent. Marilyn, on the other hand, always claimed that Cohn had invited her to spend a weekend aboard his yacht. When she refused, he snapped at her, "This is your last chance, baby." Shortly thereafter, her contract came up and Cohn refused to renew it. Whatever the circumstances, Cohn's bad decision would come back to haunt him in the form of continual criticism for not recognizing the star quality of Marilyn Monroe. Hollywood insiders claim that the irritable mogul tried to compensate for his blunder by grooming Kim Novak as his version of a blonde bombshell.

Cast adrift in Hollywood once again, Marilyn experienced several lean months. Often penniless, often hungry, she returned to modeling for some much-needed cash. The jobs, however, were few and far between. One unsavory rumor about Marilyn's attempts to stay afloat at this time claim she worked as a stripteaser in downtown Los Angeles. The rumor is likely to have originated with people who saw a young stripper named Dixie Evans, who performed at L.A.'s Mayan Theatre, and who bore a remarkable likeness to Marilyn. Evans would later exploit this resemblance by billing herself as "the Marilyn Monroe of Burlesque." Another, particularly persistent, rumor cites Marilyn as the "star" of a stag film entitled *Apples, Knockers and Cokes*; film historians have refuted this allegation. Some researchers, in fact, claim to have identified one of *Playboy* magazine's early centerfold models as the performer in question. Coincidentally, this model later became a bit player at Columbia.

Columbia boss Harry Cohn was blind to Marilyn's star quality, and allowed her option to lapse; the young actress was forced once again to rely solely on modeling. As in the past, magazine work kept Marilyn afloat financially.

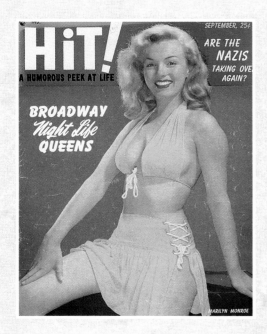

During the period in which Marilyn struggled to establish herself in the movies, her face and figure were seen on the covers of magazines from around the world. Pictured here are examples from the United States, France, Puerto Rico, and England.

Despite her lack of a studio contract, Marilyn still had the support of her agent, Harry Lipton, as well as that of Karger, Lytess, and the Carrolls. Through the efforts of one of these associates, Marilyn auditioned for producer Lester Cowan for a walk-on bit in a Marx Brothers film, *Love Happy*. Marilyn was required mainly to catch the eye of Groucho Marx (who plays a private detective) as she sidles past him. According to Marilyn, she practiced walking in front of a mirror for a week. Of the three girls who auditioned that day, it was Marilyn whom Groucho asked to repeat her interpretation of a sexy walk. Groucho approved and Marilyn landed the role. As she glides toward the camera in the slow, undulating walk that would become one of her trademarks, Marilyn's character tells Groucho, "I want you to help me . . . Some men are following me." Groucho gives his patented leer and remarks, "Really? I can't understand why!"

As a freelancer, Marilyn won a tiny but noticeable role in Love Happy, *the last film the Marx Brothers made as a team.*

Ad art, featuring Marilyn and Groucho Marx (right).

Many have attempted to explain "the walk," including Natasha Lytess, who claimed she invented it for Marilyn, as well as Emmeline Snively, who insisted it was the result of weak ankles. Gossip columnist Jimmy Starr believed Marilyn simply shaved a bit off one high heel in order to undulate in that manner, while Marilyn herself declared that she had *always* walked that way.

Love Happy is a minor, unfunny comedy that captured the Marx Brothers at the tail end of their film careers as a team. Still, Marilyn made enough of an impression on producer Cowan for him to release a publicity statement about her to columnist Louella Parsons. Cowan told Parsons that Marilyn was an orphan who had been raised in a series of foster homes in the Hollywood area. Despite the brevity of Marilyn's role in *Love Happy*, Parsons mentioned the starlet in her column. The writer became an early champion of Marilyn and later defended her on the occasions when Marilyn ran afoul of the press or her studio.

Love Happy *is a tedious effort that strains for laughs, but Marilyn's bit part showcased her stunning good looks and caught the attention of a number of influential people.*

"Golden Dreams," by photographer Tom Kelley. This evocative 1949 pinup of the sublimely beautiful Marilyn Monroe is a bona fide Hollywood legend, and one of the most celebrated photographs of all time.

Because the era's public climate—and postal regulations—were not as liberal as they would later become, this alternate version of "Golden Dreams" was also available.

Between the production of *Love Happy* in 1949 and its release in the spring of 1950, Marilyn hit her lowest point financially. With no film work on the horizon and few modeling prospects, she could not make ends meet. Desperate for cash, she agreed to pose completely nude for photographer Tom Kelley on the condition that his wife, Natalie, be present during the session. Kelley had asked Marilyn previously but she had always refused. On May 27, 1949, Marilyn posed for the calendar photograph that would one day make her a household name. She signed the release form "Mona Monroe" in a halfhearted effort to mask her identity. Kelley produced 24 transparencies of two basic poses, one a full-length profile of Marilyn lying on a swatch of red velvet, the other a seated Marilyn with her head tossed back and legs tucked beneath her. Contrary to popular belief, the full-length profile shot—entitled "A New Wrinkle"—became the original calendar photo. Only after the girl on the red velvet cloth had been identified as Marilyn Monroe did the second pose turn up. Titled "Golden Dreams," the second pose became the most exploited of the two, appearing on calendars, decks of cards, key chains, coasters, glasses, and a host of other collectibles. One entrepreneur sculpted a three-dimensional, rubberized version of "Golden Dreams," which would move suggestively at the turn of a handle. In December of 1953, "Golden Dreams" was used to launch the premiere issue of *Playboy* magazine.

Though the nude calendar shots are two of the most famous photographs in Hollywood history, Marilyn received only $50 for her efforts. Kelley himself received only a pittance when he sold the two shots to the Western Lithograph Company, but crafty manufacturers and slick promoters made a great deal of money selling bootleg versions of the calendar and other merchandise. Original sales of the calendar reached eight million copies by the mid-1950s, with millions more sold of the bootleg versions. Some of Kelley's transparencies, which had not been sold for calendar purposes, were mysteriously stolen from his studio in the early 1950s.

Shortly after she posed for Tom Kelley, Marilyn agreed to travel to New York to help promote *Love Happy*. Having always heard that New York was much cooler than Los Angeles, Marilyn packed only heavy, woolen suits to wear to the various publicity functions. Cowan and Marilyn arrived in New York in the midst of a summer heat wave. The producer graciously purchased a simple cotton dress for Marilyn, though some publicity shots show her wearing a woolen suit while eating three ice cream cones, supposedly in an effort to keep cool.

Kelley's "A New Wrinkle" was the original calendar image,
and was displayed in numberless American garages and businesses.
Like "Golden Dreams," its appeal seems timeless.

While in New York, she participated in a publicity stunt for *Photoplay* magazine, in which she presented movie fan Virginia MacAllister with a brand-new home that MacAllister had won in *Photoplay*'s "Dream House Contest." Photographs of the presentation appeared in the magazine's November 1949 issue. Nearly simultaneously, Marilyn appeared in the October 1949 issue of *Life* magazine, in which she was photographed "emoting" with seven other Hollywood starlets. Together, these articles generated some much-needed publicity for the young actress. She also landed a bit role in the forgettable Twentieth Century-Fox musical *A Ticket to Tomahawk*, though she was still working without a contract.

. . . she could just as easily swing into a pose of athletic playfulness.

By 1949, Marilyn had developed considerable versatility as a model. Adept at glamour . . .

During Marilyn's first three years in the film industry, she suffered rejection on both a professional and personal level; she sought the counsel of many who claimed to have an inside track to Hollywood success, only to be disappointed by their lack of results; she worked hard to please those who could help her; in order to pay her bills, she was forced to make sacrifices and compromises others would later criticize. Looking back over Marilyn's early film experiences, one is struck not by the glamour of Hollywood but by its harsh reality.

Fortunately, Marilyn's small bit in *Love Happy* would prove to be more of a break than she anticipated. In addition to the attention she received by promoting the film in the East, she attracted the eye of respected Hollywood agent Johnny Hyde, who saw the comedy at an advance screening. Hyde tracked down the agent of the beautiful blonde with "the walk" and negotiated with Harry Lipton to take over the contract of Marilyn Monroe. Marilyn needed an opportunity, she needed expert guidance, and she needed confidence. She would get all of that—and more—from agent Johnny Hyde.

André de Dienes captured the sportive Marilyn at Long Island's Tobey Beach in 1949.

Marilyn visited New York in 1949 to promote Love Happy. *The city was suffering a heat wave at the time, so a publicity man decided it would be fun to let Marilyn wield a clutch of cooling ice cream cones. Whimsical photos such as this were fine, but they could help a starlet's career only so much. The good news for Marilyn was that her bit in* Love Happy *had been noticed by Johnny Hyde, one of the most powerful agents in Hollywood. Her fortunes were about to take a dramatic turn for the better.*

RISING STAR

"In Hollywood a girl's virtue is much less important than her hairdo. You're judged by how you look, not by what you are. Hollywood's a place where they'll pay you a thousand dollars for a kiss, and fifty cents for your soul. I know, because I turned down the first offer enough and held out for the fifty cents."

MARILYN MONROE

Marilyn at Tobey Beach, Long Island, in the summer
of 1949. The photographer, her friend André de Dienes,
captured much of the fresh appeal and spontaneity that
would finally take hold with audiences and film
executives. Marilyn was about to begin her ascent to stardom.

*J*ohnny Hyde, an executive vice president at the prestigious William Morris Agency, met Marilyn Monroe for the first time at the Racquet Club in Palm Springs. Marilyn sensed that Hyde had more taste and refinement than most Hollywood types she had known, and she was impressed with his low-pressure style. Hyde, who was 53 when he met Marilyn, had been working for the William Morris Agency for more than 30 years. He had represented actors Howard Keel, John Hodiak, Dale Evans, and Guy Madison, but his reputation had been earned through his guidance of such big-name stars as Rita Hayworth and Betty Hutton. Marilyn and Hyde became friends almost immediately, and he began escorting the 22-year-old starlet around town to notable Hollywood establishments. Though Hyde suffered from heart disease, and his doctor had warned him to slow down, he actually accelerated his work schedule in order to firmly establish Marilyn's career.

Despite his long-time marriage to Mozelle Cravens, Johnny Hyde quickly fell in love with his beautiful and vibrant client. He repeatedly proposed marriage to Marilyn, with the promise of leaving a small fortune to her upon his death. She refused. Marilyn realized that she did not love him with the same passion he felt for her, and she did not want to take financial advantage of the relationship. Short in stature, Hyde was nonetheless a big man in Hollywood. Though Marilyn respected his opinions and his stellar reputation, she could not return his love. Marilyn later said of Hyde, "He not only knew me, he knew Norma Jeane, too. He knew all the pain and all the desperate things in me. When he put his arms around me and said he loved me, I knew it was true. Nobody had ever loved me like that. I wished with all my heart I could love him back."

Hyde steered every facet of Marilyn's life relating to her career. He arranged for her to have cosmetic surgery, including the removal of two blemishes from her chin and a slight reshaping of her nose. He hired the best hairdressers to color her hair on a regular basis, and he bought her suitable clothes for all occasions. Most importantly, he arranged for her to audition for director John Huston's searing drama *The Asphalt Jungle*. Talent scout Lucille Ryman had heard about the role during the course of her job at MGM. Always keeping an eye open for a part for Marilyn, Ryman had sent the script to Hyde, who secured the audition almost immediately.

Top Hollywood agent Johnny Hyde gave Marilyn invaluable career guidance.
He was also completely intoxicated by her, and begged her to marry him.

Marilyn worked hard to prepare for her reading with Huston. She and drama coach Natasha Lytess spent the better part of three days and nights going over her interpretation of the material. Marilyn was to read for the part of Angela Phinlay, the mistress of a crooked lawyer who participates in the planning of a jewel robbery. Because "mistress" was not a word the censors generally approved of in that era, the script referred to Angela as the lawyer's "niece."

The audition was held on a sound stage on the MGM lot. Marilyn asked Huston if she could recline on the floor for her reading as part of her interpretation of the character, and he agreed. Afterward, Marilyn requested to do it one more time. Though Huston allowed her another reading, it really wasn't necessary: He had decided to give her the role following her first attempt. Aware of all the efforts Hyde had made on Marilyn's behalf, Huston remarked, "Marilyn didn't get the part because of Johnny. She got it because she was damned good."

A small but well-written role in The Asphalt Jungle *was Marilyn's first big break. Although she is pictured here with actor Sam Jaffe . . .*

. . . her scenes were with Louis Calhern. Marilyn excelled as the naive beauty who is the mistress of a crooked lawyer.

Johnny Hyde relaxes with his favorite client. Though the agent's considerable clout made Marilyn's audition for The Asphalt Jungle *possible, she won the part by virtue of her unmistakable talent.*

Marilyn crossed paths with John Huston more than once during her career. Huston first met her during her short-lived tenure at Columbia, when he had thought of testing her for a role in a film with John Garfield. The test was called off for reasons that are not clear. Some speculate that testing an unknown actress for a single role in a specific film was too expensive, and that someone with more authority than Huston canceled the test. Others suggest that Marilyn was simply being set up for "the casting couch," and that Huston canceled the test himself when he found out. Whatever the case, Huston remembered Marilyn when she auditioned for *The Asphalt Jungle*, and he is responsible for hiring her for her first significant film role. He would also direct her last completed film, *The Misfits*—a fateful twist to her life story that could have been taken from the pages of a Hollywood script.

Marilyn's performance in Huston's film brought her critical acclaim and some favorable attention in Hollywood. A hard-bitten, gritty crime drama, *The Asphalt Jungle* was hailed for its taut direction and memorable performances by a worthy cast. Huston had a reputation for selecting actors who could give potent performances, regardless of whether or not they were stars. *The Asphalt Jungle* featured no major box-office draws but several highly regarded actors, including Sterling Hayden, Louis Calhern, Sam Jaffe, and Jean Hagen. That Marilyn held her own in this cast is a testament to her hard work and talent.

The Asphalt Jungle is classic *film noir, that genre of film that finds human conflict in the bleaker quarters of America's cities.*

Marilyn brought a subtle realism to her portrayal of the lawyer's mistress; the character's naiveté is not funny, but pathetic.

John Huston (left) was one of Hollywood's most thoughtful directors; his films are characteristically vivid and uncompromising. A filmmaker of strict standards, Huston was very pleased with Marilyn's performance in The Asphalt Jungle.

It is also a testament to Huston's genius as a director, because it was Huston who first utilized Marilyn's image to its best advantage. He understood the complexity of that image—something that escaped a number of less-talented directors Marilyn would encounter later. The storylines of a significant number of Huston's films revolve around a group of men in pursuit of a quest that ultimately fails, often because a woman lures or distracts the men from their goal. In *The Asphalt Jungle*, Marilyn's character, Angela Phinlay, isn't a bad girl; regardless, she causes the ruination of the lawyer played by Louis Calhern. His need to hold on to her as though she were a priceless possession, despite the expenses and personal risks involved, results in his downfall. The erotic innocence of Marilyn's image helped her to flesh out Angela and make her real. The girl is never painted as conniving or calculating, yet the lawyer's obsession for her is no less believable.

Its gritty nature aside, The Asphalt Jungle *took full advantage of Marilyn's good looks and unique personality.*

Marilyn with Jean Hagen and Sterling Hayden, who were convincing as doomed lovers.

Images such as this showed up in newspapers around the country, and the public began to take notice of young Marilyn Monroe.

Natasha Lytess was excited enough by her pupil's performance in *The Asphalt Jungle* to resign her job at Columbia and become Marilyn's personal acting coach. Hollywood insiders who had thought that Johnny Hyde's unwavering faith in Marilyn was unwarranted began to look at her in a different light. Still, no handsome offers from the major studios were forthcoming. In another of those twists of fate that seem to characterize Marilyn's life, former husband Jim Dougherty, by that time a Los Angeles policeman, was assigned to keep the fans behind the barricades at Grauman's Egyptian Theater, where *The Asphalt Jungle* premiered. He watched the celebrities as they got out of their limousines, hoping to catch a glimpse of Norma Jeane Dougherty. He did not know that Marilyn had been advised by Hyde not to attend the premiere. It was not really Norma Jeane that Jim Dougherty would have seen anyway.

Just before *The Asphalt Jungle* was released, Marilyn found work in two minor films distributed by MGM: a prizefight drama entitled *Right Cross*, and *Hometown Story*, an industrial film financed by General Motors. Marilyn was cast in the former as a model with the unlikely name of Dusky Ledoux. She uttered only a few trivial lines in her single scene, a brief dinner-date bit with star Dick Powell.

Hometown Story, which was never released commercially, featured Marilyn as Miss Martin, a secretary in a newspaper office. One of *Hometown Story*'s few public showings was at the Loew's Metropolitan in Brooklyn in June 1950. After that, this hour-long propaganda film for American industry did not surface again until 1962, when it was released in Australia as a Monroe oddity. Because of her success in *The Asphalt Jungle*, and her brief appearances in *Right Cross* and *Hometown Story*, Marilyn was hoping for a contract from MGM, but none was offered.

Marilyn's bit part in Right Cross *let her play opposite popular leading man Dick Powell, but the picture was a minor one.*

In addition to these films, Marilyn took a bit part in a Mickey Rooney vehicle entitled *The Fireball*. Rooney's career was at low ebb at this time, as the energetic actor struggled through a bleak period a few years before the first of his famous comebacks. *The Fireball*, a lightweight story of a roller-skating star, attracted very little notice and did nothing to further Marilyn's career.

Even the ever-energetic Mickey Rooney (far right) could not salvage The Fireball, *a tired programmer about professional roller skaters. Marilyn's part was tiny.*

The Asphalt Jungle *did not catapult Marilyn into major films. To the contrary,* Hometown Story *was not even intended for general theatrical release. Marilyn, seen here with character actor Alan Hale, Jr., was fetching in a small part as a secretary.*

Marilyn's other notable effort from this period was a television commercial for the Union Oil Company of California. In a provocative voice, Marilyn introduces her car, "Cynthia," and expresses her confidence in Union Oil's Royal Triton gasoline, the only gas good enough for Cynthia's "little tummy." The commercial was aired in California during the 1950-51 television season.

Marilyn actually worked a great deal in 1950 because of the efforts of Johnny Hyde, but both were striving for the security of a lucrative contract from a major studio. Hyde took an important step toward that goal by securing for Marilyn a role in Joseph Mankiewicz's enormously successful adaptation of *All About Eve*, a sharply cynical look at theater life. Marilyn's role was slightly smaller than her part had been in *The Asphalt Jungle*, but Hyde convinced her of the wisdom of appearing in a small role in a film by a major director rather than in a larger role in a film directed by a minor talent.

Marilyn's only television commercial is an amusing 1950 trifle for a California oil company. Her breathless delivery of the spot's inane dialogue is almost a parody of the dumb-blonde image she would eventually struggle to escape.

Hyde proved to be correct, as Marilyn's part was pivotal to the narrative of *All About Eve*. Her character, Miss Caswell—an empty-headed actress who, according to one character, graduated from "the Copacabana School of Dramatic Art"—has no pretense about using her beauty and her body to get a break in the theater. Miss Caswell provides a counterpoint to the more cunning Eve (Anne Baxter), who uses underhanded tricks to get to the top. After Eve is exposed for the cruel manipulator that she is, Miss Caswell's more obvious methods are seen as almost honest in comparison. As she had done in *The Asphalt Jungle*, Marilyn made a strong impression amidst a powerfully talented cast: Baxter, Bette Davis, George Sanders, and Celeste Holm. Darryl F. Zanuck of Twentieth Century-Fox was impressed enough with Marilyn's interpretation of Miss Caswell to offer her another screen test and the chance for another contract.

Marilyn found herself in some fast company in All About Eve. *From left, Anne Baxter, Bette Davis, Marilyn, George Sanders.*

Near the end of 1950, then, Marilyn returned to the sound stages of Twentieth Century-Fox for a second screen test. This time the test was done with sound, and Marilyn was given a scene to do with another actor. The scene involved a dispute between a gangster and his girlfriend, with established actor Richard Conte playing opposite Marilyn. In an interview conducted shortly before his death in 1975, Conte recalled Marilyn as a serious actress whose acting style looked quite natural on screen. Their scene had involved a tense, emotional confrontation, and Conte remembered Marilyn's total concentration on her character. Perhaps as a token of good luck, or as a reminder to Fox executives of her recent series of roles, Marilyn wore the same dress for her screen test as she had worn in *The Fireball, Hometown Story*, and in the last scene of *All About Eve*.

All About Eve *provided Marilyn*
with another small but noticeable part in a prestigious film.
Her interpretation of the ambitious Miss Caswell
is at once amusing and believable.

Zanuck viewed the test in December of 1950 and requested that Marilyn be put under a six-month contract immmediately. When reminded that she had been under contract once before and dropped, he roared, "I don't care. Bring her back." Marilyn closed her second deal with Fox on December 10, 1950.

The Fox contract was probably the last piece of business Johnny Hyde helped negotiate for Marilyn. Just about the time she signed with the studio, Hyde entered Cedars of Lebanon Hospital after complaining of breathing difficulties. Though released a few days later and sent to Palm Springs to recuperate, the end was near for the prominent agent. On December 17, Hyde suffered a serious heart attack and died the next day. Supposedly, his last intelligible words were about Marilyn.

Re-signed by Twentieth Century-Fox at the end of 1950, Marilyn was plunged into a fresh round of studio publicity photos.

Very quickly, photo editors and moviegoers became aware of Marilyn's "flesh impact"—the way in which her presence radiated from still photos and movie screens with remarkable immediacy.

The Hyde family, including Johnny's sons, ex-wife, and brother, were brutal in their treatment of Marilyn, whom they blamed for the breakup of their home. Through various channels, they let her know that she would not be welcome at the funeral. Some of Hyde's closest associates urged her to go if she wanted to, and Marilyn decided to attend with a couple of his business friends. There she broke down completely, throwing herself on the casket and sobbing Johnny's name.

Marilyn was inconsolable at Hyde's death and grew increasingly despondent in the days after the funeral. Staying with Natasha Lytess during this painful period, she remained in her room most of the time. One day Lytess returned home to find a distressing note from Marilyn on her pillow: "I leave my car and fur stole to Natasha." Lytess discovered Marilyn in her bedroom, unconscious from swallowing a bottle of sleeping pills. Fortunately Lytess had arrived in time to avert disaster. This was Marilyn's second, or possibly third, attempt at suicide, setting up an alarming pattern of disappointment, depression, and self-destruction that would haunt the actress in the years to follow.

Fox emphasized the glamorous aspect of Marilyn's nature . . .

. . . but the real woman was more concerned with weightier matters.
Note the framed photograph (left) of the great actress
Eleonora Duse, whom Marilyn idolized.

Moments from 1949-50.
Above is a particularly striking photo from André de Dienes's
memorable Tobey Beach session. Not merely beautiful,
Marilyn glows with health and good cheer.

*Splash! Marilyn whips the
sea into a froth . . .*

*. . . and later settles
back for her own brand
of yard work.*

*Master of all she
surveys? Not quite
yet . . .*

*. . . but Marilyn's star
was definitely on the
rise.*

Marilyn found some solace in her career, which had finally developed far enough to bring her a measure of financial security. Fox put her to work almost immediately in the comedy *As Young as You Feel*. The picture was tailored to the talents of character actor Monty Woolley, but Zanuck asked the scriptwriter, Lamar Trotti, to flesh out Marilyn's character without changing the role. Marilyn portrayed Harriet, a secretary for a corporation that forces Woolley's character to retire at age 65 because of company policy. *As Young as You Feel* garnered good reviews and a healthy box office at the time of its release. Bosley Crowther, a well-known reviewer for *The New York Times*, noted, "Quite as refreshing as the story is the manner in which it is played, with the whole cast working adroitly as a selfless and perfectly balanced team." Crowther singled out Marilyn's portrayal of Harriet as "superb."

An exuberant meeting of curves and right angles.

In the early part of 1951, Marilyn's spirits were lifted by two incidents, both of which gained recognition for the young actress with the movie-going public. A color photo of her was featured in *Life* magazine, and she was asked to be a presenter at the Academy Awards ceremony. Her inclusion as a presenter was probably based on her appearance in *All About Eve*—one of the most prominent feature films of the previous year. Marilyn presented the Oscar for outstanding achievement in sound recording to Thomas T. Moulton for his work on *All About Eve*.

Marilyn won good notices for her performance as a secretary in
As Young as You Feel. *Here, she shares a scene with Albert Dekker,*
one of Hollywood's top character actors of the 1940s and '50s.

In addition to her film assignments, Marilyn was required once again to pose endlessly for publicity photos. Sometimes these photos were inspired by a specific stunt or event. Once Marilyn was chastised by a female newspaper columnist for wearing a low-cut red dress to a party at the Beverly Hills Hotel. According to Marilyn, the columnist called her cheap and vulgar. Not stopping there, the writer then suggested that the actress would look better in a potato sack. The studio publicity department capitalized on the story by shooting some stills of Marilyn in a form-fitting, burlap potato sack. The photos were published in newspapers throughout the country. As a result, a potato farm in Idaho sent Marilyn a bag of potatos. Marilyn recalled, "There was a potato shortage on then, and the boys in publicity stole them all. I never saw one. It just goes to show why I always ask, 'Can you trust a publicity man or can't you?'"

Regardless of whether the photos Marilyn posed for were directly related to her films or just for general release, she used her experience as a model to wonderful advantage. Marilyn's studio pinups attracted the attention of servicemen, film fans, and newspaper editors from around the world. Requests for photos of Marilyn quickly exceeded those for any other Fox star. Darryl F. Zanuck suspected that someone who knew Marilyn was tampering with the mail tabulations on her behalf. When he realized that this was not the case, he began assigning her to any film he felt called for a gorgeous blonde.

The Fox publicity department was particularly inspired when it came up with this priceless outfit.

The boys in publicity kept grinding away. Marilyn prepares for a little ice skating . . .

. . . then gets ready to bag a big one.

In about 1951, Marilyn visited Van Nuys High School, where she gave pointers to students "on attaining success in life."

Zanuck realized that publicity and the right roles would make Marilyn's image and personality not only useful but profitable. But many believe that Zanuck had no faith or interest in her as a serious actress; Marilyn herself had no illusions about Zanuck's opinion of her acting ability. Consequently, what Zanuck considered "the right roles" were endless variations on the Miss Caswell character—the buxom blonde who was both sexually attractive and amusingly naive. But contrary to the opinions of many Monroe biographers, not all of these films were "bad." A few, such as *As Young as You Feel*, received good reviews at the time of their release and performed adequately at the box office. However, these films were not the big-budgeted productions that Hollywood and the public considered star material. In addition, Marilyn was cast in secondary roles that became virtually interchangable from film to film.

Fox boss Darryl Zanuck had little interest in developing Marilyn as a serious actress. In his mind, Marilyn's profit potential was directly linked to her image as a glamour girl.

Marilyn was sexy, all right, but she knew that a relentless emphasis on her face and figure could severely limit her career.

Love Nest was Marilyn's second feature under her new Fox contract. In this minor comedy about the day-to-day happenings in a small apartment building, Marilyn portrays a former WAC named Bobbie who disrupts the marriage of June Haver and William Lundigan. The film is memorable not only for Marilyn's presence but also for the participation of prominent screenwriter I.A.L. Diamond, who later partnered with writer-director Billy Wilder, a man Marilyn would come to know well in the years ahead.

Television personality Jack Paar had a secondary role in *Love Nest*; he is one of the few of her costars from this period who has spoken unkindly of her. Paar has commented that he saw Marilyn carry around several books by Marcel Proust while on the set, but he claims that she never read one. Paar has said also that her attempts to become well read were mere pretensions, remarking that "beneath the facade of Marilyn there was only a frightened waitress in a diner."

Paar's opinion—although echoed by other people through the years—lacks credibility. He apparently did not know that during the production of *Love Nest*, Marilyn was enrolled in the adult extension program at the University of California at Los Angeles. While at UCLA, she took courses in literature and art appreciation. Marilyn was bright and intellectually ambitious. Her only "failing" in this regard was that she was untutored, a condition that she took pains to correct.

A Love Nest *lobby card. Note the prominence of Marilyn's billing.*

June Haver remembered that Marilyn's physical presence "stunned" the Love Nest *crew and sent them into "sheer shock." Against all odds, then, costar Jack Paar (above) claimed to have found Marilyn "pretty tiresome."*

Marilyn, with June Haver, in a scene from Love Nest. *Haver, a popular Fox star at the time, later recalled that "Marilyn had that electric something. . . ."*

Marilyn blossoms for the camera,
in a gown calculated to attract more than just honeybees.

Let's Make It Legal, originally titled *Don't Call Me Mother*, was released shortly after *Love Nest* and featured Marilyn as a voluptuous golddigger who hunts for a wealthy husband at a luxury hotel. Reviews of this film were not kind; *Time* magazine called *Let's Make It Legal* "one of 1951's worst comedies." The critics were less harsh regarding Marilyn's physical appearance, and any positive commentary regarding the film focused on her striking beauty or remarkable shape. This reception did suggest a sort of progress, but Marilyn began to tire of these secondary roles in minor comedies—parts that she was often handed as an afterthought.

Marilyn and Let's Make It Legal *costar Zachary Scott.*

Despite an accomplished cast,
Let's Make It Legal *does not rise above transparent romantic comedy.*
From left, Barbara Bates, Macdonald Carey, Claudette Colbert,
Zachary Scott, and Marilyn.

The Russian character actor and teacher Michael Chekhov was an important early influence on Marilyn as she strove to grow as an actress. In her personal gallery of heroes, Chekhov ranked very high.

Troubled, she went to the William Morris Agency for support and advice. Those at William Morris who had known Johnny Hyde were cool toward her, perhaps even blaming her for his death. No one there had any interest in helping her with her career. She called her former agent, Harry Lipton, for advice, and he suggested that she see Hugh French at the Famous Artists Agency. French agreed to become her agent, though he and Marilyn would never have the close personal relationship that she and Johnny Hyde had. Their association was always strictly professional. When Marilyn's contract was up in May 1951, French helped negotiate the renewal, extending her term at Fox from six months to seven years.

Despite French's efforts on his new client's behalf, it was probably Marilyn's sensational appearance at the Fox exhibitors' party in the spring of 1951 that helped land her a seven-year contract. In attendance that evening were such famous movie stars as Susan Hayward, Tyrone Power, Gregory Peck, June Haver, and Jeanne Crain. Marilyn not only upstaged these Hollywood luminaries but also secured a seat at the table of Fox president Spyros Skouras. Arriving late and somewhat out of breath, Marilyn made a true Hollywood entrance, stealing attention from more prominent stars. The exhibitors (the owners and operators of movie theaters across America) promptly turned their attention to Marilyn, clamoring to know which movies she was scheduled to star in. A reporter for *Collier's* magazine captured the effect of her entrance: "Amid a slowly gathering hush, she stood there, a blond apparition in a strapless cocktail gown, a little breathless as if she were Cinderella, just stepped from the pumpkin coach."

After attaining a seven-year commitment from Fox, Marilyn's film roles did get better. Though still not cast in starring roles, she received juicier supporting parts in films by more notable directors. To improve her skills in the hopes of upgrading her roles, Marilyn enrolled in an acting course with Michael Chekhov, a Russian character actor who had actually studied under the legendary Stanislavski. Chekhov had been recommended to Marilyn by actor Jack Palance. Like Marilyn, Palance had feared he was being typecast in the industry and had sought out a teacher who could improve his overall acting skills. Marilyn arranged to study with Chekhov in the fall of 1951. Her tenure as Chekhov's pupil provides an early example of her inclination toward Method acting, in which the actor attempts to personally experience or live out the emotional content of his role. This interest would culminate in her tutelage under Lee Strasberg at the Actors Studio during the mid-1950s.

In addition to her classes with Chekhov, Marilyn continued to work under the guidance of Natasha Lytess. Beginning with *Clash by Night,* Lytess coached Marilyn on the set of her films, much to the chagrin of her directors and costars. Fox had loaned Marilyn to RKO Pictures for *Clash by Night* (an act of largesse that Fox executives would not repeat after Marilyn became a star). Based on a play by Clifford Odets, *Clash by Night* represented a considerable improvement over the pictures Marilyn had been assigned at Fox. Directed by Fritz Lang, the film was a moody melodrama about a woman who tries to settle down with an honest, hard-working fisherman but is attracted to the excitement offered by a more aggressive younger man. Barbara Stanwyck was selected for the starring role, with Paul Douglas, Robert Ryan, and Keith Andes rounding out the cast. Marilyn portrayed Peggy, a worker in a fish cannery who is engaged to the character played by Andes. A working-class girl in a gritty, slice-of-life setting, Peggy was far less glamorous than the characters Marilyn had been playing. The character also had a no-nonsense independence of spirit that Marilyn had never before had a chance to express on the screen. The young actress was essentially cast against type—and effectively so—for one of the few times in her career.

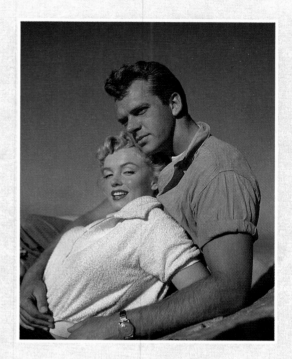

Marilyn's best scenes in Clash by Night *were opposite rugged actor Keith Andes. The film was an important career break for both of the young performers.*

Clash By Night *is one of the best of Marilyn's early films.*
As in The Asphalt Jungle *and* All About Eve,
she proved her ability to keep pace with a potent
ensemble cast. In this scene, she knocks back a beer with costar Robert Ryan.

Clash by Night *was directed by German expatriate Fritz Lang,
who was known for powerful films filled with tough, driven characters.
Marilyn and Keith Andes were appealingly effective as Peggy and Joe,
an uncomplicated working-class couple.*

Fritz Lang, a noted director in the German silent cinema before making a name for himself in Hollywood, fought constantly with Marilyn and Lytess over the latter's presence throughout the shoot. He attempted to bar Lytess from his set, but Marilyn objected to Lang's order and complained to studio executives. Eventually, a compromise was reached but not before the incident caused bad feelings among Marilyn, Lang, and Lytess. Costar Paul Douglas was another person who resented Marilyn's insistence on having her coach close by. The veteran actor also was irked by Marilyn's constant tardiness. Barbara Stanwyck, on the other hand, was generally tolerant of Marilyn's behavior, recognizing her insecurity among a cast of movie veterans. Though the production of the film was not a comfortable experience, Marilyn garnered good reviews for her role, and *Clash by Night* did a smashing business at the box office.

Peggy's relationship with her boyfriend is roughly physical, and she reacts to the bit of domination shown above by hauling off and socking her fella on the jaw. To Marilyn, the character's vigor must have been sweet relief after the succession of two-dimensional glamour-girl roles.

One of the reasons for that box office success was undoubtedly due to the publicity blitz that occurred when wire-service reporter Aline Mosby discovered that Marilyn Monroe had posed nude for a calendar photo. Mosby found out about the calendar in February 1952, possibly through a clandestine tip from *Clash* producer Jerry Wald. The following month, she interviewed Marilyn about the circumstances surrounding the photo session. At first, Fox executives were frantic over the discovery and urged Marilyn to deny everything. Others advised her to admit the truth, a decision Marilyn opted for because she saw no reason to be ashamed of what she had done. In her interview with Mosby, Marilyn simply told the truth about why she had posed nude: "I was broke and needed the money." Though some reporters seemed shocked, the press was generally delighted with her candor and wit about the incident. The publicity proved a boon for RKO's *Clash by Night*, which opened in limited release during the same month Mosby made the fateful discovery.

The release of Marilyn's calendar story to the press and public has become one of the most widely told tales of her career, and biographers seem almost compelled to embellish it. Because the story worked to Marilyn's advantage in terms of attracting sympathetic attention without damaging her career, some have claimed that Fox officials tipped Mosby off about the photos, or that Marilyn herself did it. Whatever the specifics of the incident, exactly *why* Marilyn got away with such a potentially scandalous escapade is rarely touched upon.

Today, the decade of the 1950s is remembered as conservative and naive. That perception tells only part of the story. In truth, the era had an undercurrent of conflict and turmoil in which issues of sex, racial inequality, and other controversial topics began to be openly discussed. A franker attitude toward sexuality, particularly as it related to women, was signaled by the release of the Kinsey report on female sexuality just a few months after the calendar story broke. Then, in December of 1953, the first issue of *Playboy*—a magazine that would quickly become famous for its open attitude toward sex and nudity—hit America's newsstands with a photo of Marilyn on the cover and a reproduction of one of her calendar photos as the centerfold.

Marilyn's image seemed to embody the contradictory viewpoints on sex that existed in that era. Overtly sensual, Marilyn was also demure, natural, and honest—almost innocent—about her sexuality. The calendar story captured all of these delightful contradictions perfectly. Given this increasing fascination with sexual freedom in a society still labeled conservative, Marilyn's success over the next few years is no coincidence. That she found herself trapped by her image during this period should be no surprise.

Marilyn was surrounded by a barrage of publicity for the rest of 1952. In May, she had her appendix removed. Preparing to operate, the doctor found a handwritten note attached to her stomach that read, "Please take only what you have to. And please, please, no major scars." Marilyn received get-well greetings from thousands of fans, and publicity photos of her recuperation were released to the press.

Audiences of the 1950s were fascinated by Marilyn's unique mix of provocative sexuality and fresh-faced innocence.

Well-wishers sent flowers as Marilyn recovered from an appendectomy at L.A.'s Cedars of Lebanon Hospital.

Marilyn's operation wasn't the only thing that excited the public's interest in her at this time. Just prior to her hospitalization, a reporter had discovered that Marilyn's mother was confined to a state mental hospital. Marilyn had always allowed the press to believe that both of her parents were dead. When the discovery was made, she again told the truth, explaining that she had never really known Gladys Baker and did not want to put the vulnerable woman in the spotlight. When her parentage became public knowledge, Marilyn removed Gladys from the state facility and moved her to Rockhaven, a private sanitarium in Verdugo, California. The rising star with a rising income also acquired a business manager, Inez Melson, who was appointed conservator of Gladys's estate. Marilyn visited her mother at Rockhaven only occasionally, but she took financial responsibility for her care until her own death in 1962. At that time, her estate met this need.

Not all of the publicity surrounding Marilyn at this time was of a shocking nature, or a "hot scoop." In April 1952, Marilyn appeared on the cover of *Life* magazine for the first time. The magazine had sent photographer Philippe Halsman to Hollywood with a list of young actresses to profile in the hopes of getting an eye-catching photo essay. Halsman suggested to the magazine that Marilyn be added to the list. He had photographed her for *Life* in 1949 for the "Eight Girls Try Out Mixed Emotions" article, and he knew her increasing popularity was due in part to the efforts of photographers. Halsman decided to photograph Marilyn in her apartment in a variety of situations. While there, he noticed a bookcase filled with such books as *The Story of Fabian Socialism* and *The Negro in American Literature.* He also observed a few framed photographs, including one of 19th-century actress Eleonora Duse. Thinking the books and photos an affectation, Halsman asked Marilyn about Duse. To his surprise, she revealed a depth of knowledge about the legendary actress. The photographer also noticed a pair of dumbbells lying on the floor. Marilyn said she used the weights to strengthen her torso and flatten her stomach.

Halsman's photos of Marilyn were sensational enough for *Life*'s editors to center the whole story around her and to put her on the cover. The article intoned, "Every so often, more in hope than conviction, Hollywood announces the advent of a sensational new glamour girl, guaranteed to entice people from all lands to the box office. Usually the sensation fizzles. But today the most respected studio seers, in a crescendo of talk unparalleled since the debut of Rita Hayworth, are saying that the genuine article is here at last: a sturdy blonde named Marilyn Monroe."

A photograph from the Philippe Halsman session that produced this seductive image adorned the cover of the April 7, 1952, issue of Life *magazine.*

Cast as a beauty queen, Marilyn costarred with David Wayne in a lighthearted segment of the episodic comedy We're Not Married.

The great character actor Charles Laughton played opposite Marilyn in one segment of O. Henry's Full House.

Later that year, an article in *Time* magazine profiled Marilyn, the most talked-about starlet in Hollywood, and claimed that she was receiving over 5,000 letters a week from "smitten admirers." Soldiers stationed on the Aleutian Islands voted her "the girl most likely to thaw out Alaska," while a whole battalion in Korea volunteered to marry her. Students in the 7th Divisional Medical Corps elected her "the girl they would most like to examine." The article also commented on the effect her popularity and publicity had had on the box-office tally of her latest films. Some exhibitors showing *Clash by Night,* for example, were luring more fans to their theaters by putting Marilyn's name at the top of the marquee, instead of star Barbara Stanwyck's. The article also offered some of Marilyn's oft-repeated quotes: When asked if she really had nothing on in the famous calendar photos, Marilyn replied, "I had the radio on." When asked what she wore to bed, Marilyn said with a straight face, "Chanel No. 5." Marilyn courted the members of the press, playing them as a skilled musician plays an instrument. The *Time* magazine article and similar ones—combining anecdotes about Marilyn's popularity with her witty remarks—reinforced her image as a hot blonde bombshell who was disarmingly guileless.

The publicity blitz that surrounded Marilyn in 1952 generated respectable box-office receipts for all of her films released that year. After *Clash by Night,* she appeared in secondary roles in a handful of films released by Fox, most of them comedies. *We're Not Married* featured Marilyn and costar David Wayne as one of five couples who discover they were never legally married. The anthology film *O. Henry's Full House* contained adaptations of five separate stories by American writer O. Henry. In Marilyn's episode, entitled "The Cop and the Anthem," she portrays a young, sensitive streetwalker opposite the renowned Charles Laughton. Marilyn compared the experience of working with Laughton to having an audience with God, though she and the mighty actor got along quite well. Despite the film's respectable literary source, it was not well received, primarily due to the uneven quality of the different episodes.

The best of this modest series of films is probably *Monkey Business,* a madcap screwball comedy directed by Howard Hawks. Marilyn is featured as Charles Coburn's secretary, Lois Laurel. One of the picture's running gags is Lois's complete lack of secretarial skills, and that she has been hired only for her obvious physical attributes. Coburn repeatedly barks to Marilyn, "Find someone to type this!" Cary Grant and Ginger Rogers starred in *Monkey Business,* which was written by top-notch scriptwriters Ben Hecht, I.A.L. Diamond, and Charles Lederer.

Monkey Business *cast Marilyn as a good-looking but incompetent secretary.*
Although peripheral to the main action of the plot,
Marilyn made the most of her amusing scenes with star Cary Grant.

Though none of these comedies were considered major releases, most of them feature big-name actors and the handiwork of well-respected directors and scriptwriters—a step up from the quality of films Marilyn had appeared in just the year before. Despite her continued disappointment over the caliber of her roles, Marilyn was more secure in the industry at this juncture than she had ever been in the past. There was a logical progression to her career after she landed her second Fox contract, though Marilyn was worried—and rightly so—about the sameness of her roles.

Don't Bother to Knock *was a milestone in Marilyn's career because it marked her first attempt at a heavily dramatic starring role. This lobby card shows her with costar Richard Widmark and child actress Donna Corcoran.*

Marilyn got the opportunity she had been waiting for with the drama *Don't Bother to Knock*, which was released a few months before *Monkey Business* but made at roughly the same time. Cast in the starring role as Nell, a psychotic babysitter who threatens to harm the innocent little girl left in her charge, Marilyn attempted to make use of her training and hard work to deliver a good performance—and perhaps deliver herself from a succession of "dumb blonde" characters. Richard Widmark costarred as a stranger whom Nell mistakes for her dead lover. Nell's confusion over past and present events pushes her over the edge and becomes the catalyst for her actions against the child.

Marilyn's performance as Nell, a mentally disturbed babysitter, is mannered but strangely effective.

Marilyn portrayed Nell as being desperately melancholy, rather than overtly menacing. Seen here with Marilyn and Richard Widmark is costar Anne Bancroft, making her film debut.

Lively publicity photos pit Marilyn against actress Lurene Tuttle, cast as the mother of the endangered little girl.

Unfortunately, neither the scriptwriter nor the director provided Marilyn with much to work with in terms of understanding and developing the character of Nell. The script offered only the vaguest suggestion for the causes of Nell's mental imbalance and provided no credible account of the weaknesses in her personality that might have led to insanity. Roy Ward Baker, a competent but not outstanding director, offered Marilyn no key with which she might have unlocked the mysteries behind Nell. According to some of her later directors, Marilyn often needed that sort of insight in order to come to grips with her characters' motivations, and to play a role convincingly. She received no help of that kind during the shooting of *Don't Bother to Knock*.

Consequently, most of the reviews of her performance were brutal. Bosley Crowther of *The New York Times*, who had recognized Marilyn's potential in earlier films, summed up the tone of many reviews when he wrote, "All the equipment that Miss Monroe has to handle the job are a childishly blank expression and a provokingly feeble, hollow voice." Other reviewers mocked her attempt at a dramatic role. Archer Winsten of the *New York Post* quipped, "In *Don't Bother to Knock* at the Globe, they've thrown Marilyn Monroe into the deep dramatic waters, sink or swim, and while she doesn't really do either, you might say that she floats. With that figure, what else can she do . . . ."

The low-key style of Richard Widmark helped to prevent Don't Bother to Knock *from going over the top. Still . . .*

. . . the film does have its share of melodrama, as in this scene, in which the babysitter threatens to brain her well-meaning uncle, played by Elisha Cook, Jr.

Dispelling these negative perceptions of Marilyn's performance in the film is this testimony to her skills by costar Anne Bancroft: "It was a remarkable experience. Because it was one of those very few times in all my experiences in Hollywood when I felt that give and take that can only happen when you are working with good actors. There was just this scene of one woman seeing another woman who was helpless and in pain, and [Marilyn] was helpless and in pain. It was so real, I responded. I really reacted to her. She moved me so that tears came into my eyes."

In addition to her dramatic role in *Don't Bother to Knock*, Marilyn starred in the "Statement in Full" episode of the NBC radio program *Hollywood Star Playhouse* in August 1952. She was cast as a scheming murderess, a character that foreshadowed her role as Rose Loomis in *Niagara*—the film that would finally allow her to fulfill her hard-fought goal of being a genuine movie star.

No matter how dramatically intense Marilyn's roles might become, the familiar glamour was never far away.

*Marilyn did dramatic radio just once,
on the August 31, 1952, installment of NBC's* Hollywood Star Playhouse.
*Her part as a murderess foreshadowed her next film role—the one
that would propel her to undisputed stardom.*

GODDESS

Marilyn: "It was so wonderful, Joe. You've never heard such cheering."

Joe: "Yes, I have."

MARILYN MONROE TO JOE DIMAGGIO,
AFTER ENTERTAINING THE TROOPS IN KOREA, 1954

Poised on the brink of worldwide fame and adulation,
Marilyn strikes a provocative pose
in the Hollywood Hills, circa 1953.

*P*roducer Charles Brackett wanted to do a film against the dynamic backdrop of Niagara Falls and summoned writers Walter Reisch and Richard Breen to work up a suitable script based on his ideas. As devised by these veteran screenwriters, the plot was perfect to display not only Marilyn's talents as a dramatic actress but also her image as a blonde bombshell. Shot on location in the late spring and summer of 1952, *Niagara* was directed by Henry Hathaway, a competent craftsman who had built a secure reputation in Hollywood with straightforward, unpretentious films. Marilyn starred as a cunning adulteress named Rose Loomis, a character much harsher than those she had played in her earlier films.

Niagara *not only assured Marilyn's stardom, it gave her the only opportunity she would have to play an out-and-out villainess. The character, Rose Loomis, is memorably wicked. This unusual publicity shot of Marilyn and costar Joseph Cotten sums up much of the film's fascinating sexual tension.*

Left: *The wronged husband takes justice into his own hands.* Below: *Marilyn confers with the director of* Niagara, *Henry Hathaway.*

Niagara revolves around Rose's plot to murder her neurotic husband, George, who suffers painful memories of his war experiences. Rose uses her young lover, played by Richard Allan, to carry out her plan. Joseph Cotten costarred as George, who—like Rose—is an unsympathetic yet oddly likable character. Jean Peters and Casey Adams rounded out the cast as a honeymooning couple caught up in the intrigue of Rose's plan.

Left: *The film's bell-tower sequence is a small masterpiece of lighting and design.* Above: *Marilyn croons "Kiss" to Jean Peters and Casey Adams.*

Rose Loomis exhibits none of the naiveté that was a key element of Marilyn's image; the character uses her sexual attractiveness and her bold good looks to manipulate her husband and lover into doing what she wants. Rose's effect on men is symbolized by the famous sequence in which Marilyn was photographed from behind briskly walking in her undulating, hip-swaying fashion. Actually, the picture features three walking sequences; the one that received the most attention is often referred to as "the longest walk in cinema history"—116 feet of film of Marilyn in a black skirt and red sweater walking away from the camera into the distance. In a daring shot for the era, the camera eye remains firmly focused on Marilyn's swaying posterior.

The variety of form-fitting outfits worn by Marilyn in Niagara *took on added dimension when the star swung into the famous "Monroe walk."*

Then there is the famous red dress, a clinging, low-cut dazzler that Marilyn wore when she crooned the song "Kiss." When the character played by Casey Adams spies Rose's entrance in this dress, he remarks to his wife, "Get out the fire hose!" Millions of moviegoers shared that sentiment.

An original Niagara *lobby card, featuring (from left) Russell Collins, Marilyn, and costars Jean Peters and Casey Adams.*

Of all the stunning outfits Marilyn wore in her films, none are as startling in their impact as the red dress she wore in Niagara.

"Would you mind playing this?" Though "Kiss" was not the first song Marilyn sang on screen, it may well be the steamiest.

Interestingly, though the filmmakers undoubtedly realized the box-office potential for *Niagara* because of the publicity surrounding Marilyn's wardrobe and lingering views of her undulating body, the film did not exploit Marilyn as much as it *showcased* her. The walking sequences and the sexy outfits were essential to the film's plot because they demonstrated Rose's effect on men—her power to persuade them into actions they might not otherwise consider.

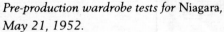
Pre-production wardrobe tests for Niagara, *May 21, 1952.*

Niagara is filled with clever touches that enhance the story and capture the dynamic quality of Rose Loomis. The character represents pure sexuality. If water is a literary symbol for woman, then to place Rose against the roaring backdrop of Niagara Falls is to imply that she is "all woman." It is no coincidence that both Rose's husband and lover die by going over the Falls. The association between Rose and the Falls was made complete by one of the poster ads for the film, which depicts a larger-than-life Marilyn lying atop the Falls with the water flowing over her scantily clad body. As much a natural wonder as the Falls themselves, Rose consistently wears clothes that are variations of black and red—two colors associated with women who are alluring, cunning, and powerful. Clever set design contrasts Rose's open sexuality and lust for life with George's worrisome, neurotic behavior: Rose is associated with wide open spaces while George hides himself in closed, cramped quarters. The role of Rose Loomis was tailored to take advantage of the sexual nature of Marilyn's image, yet gave her a valuable opportunity to stretch her rapidly developing acting skills.

Right *and* below right: *Marilyn Monroe and Niagara Falls: the momentous meeting of two great natural wonders.* Below left: *Marilyn and Richard Allan share an illicit kiss.*

Despite the melodramatic plot, *Niagara* was a tightly woven combination of excellent casting, taut direction, and clever production design. Touting the film's strong points in most reviews, the critics deemed the film a success and singled out Marilyn for her performance. Often, however, reviewers complimented her in a backhanded way, acknowledging her powerful presence yet maintaining that "Miss Monroe is not the perfect actress at this point," or that she "is not an actress, heaven knows." This type of remark would characterize critical reaction to Marilyn's work throughout her career. Reviewers were unable to understand that her use of her physical attributes to express aspects of a character was as much an acting skill as the ability to convincingly deliver dialogue.

Critics may have had their doubts about Marilyn, but the public made her a full-fledged star after the release of *Niagara* in January 1953. The film grossed over six million dollars that year, a tidy sum for the era. After many years of struggle, Marilyn had at last attained her goal. But at that time, as always, she understood perfectly who was responsible for her success. Marilyn commented, ". . . I want to say that the people—if I am a star—the people made me a star; no studio, no person, but the people did."

On location at Niagara Falls. Note the enormous size of the Technicolor camera.

A montage of scenes from
Niagara. *Rose meets the
resort's new guest . . .*

*. . . and later makes
small talk with the woman
and her husband.*

*The police think Rose's
husband is dead, but Rose
knows better . . .*

*. . . which prompts her to
try to get on the first bus
to anywhere.*

*But the border is blocked
and Rose is trapped.
Frightened, she runs . . .*

*. . . to a shadowed
bell tower, where her
luck finally runs out.*

During the production of *Niagara*, the press began to compare Marilyn to Jean Harlow, the famous blonde sex symbol of the Depression era. After the film's release, the comparisons between Monroe and Harlow intensified. Typical of this sort of commentary was an article by Erskine Johnson in the *New York World Telegram & Sun* titled "Marilyn Inherits Harlow's Mantle." Johnson wrote: "Hollywood took 14 years, three-score screen tests and a couple of million dollars to find a successor to Jean Harlow. . . ." Aside from their platinum blonde hair, Jean Harlow and Marilyn Monroe did share some common characterisics. Both were able to project a healthy sexuality on the screen, without appearing vulgar or artificial. Publicity for both of the actresses emphasized their sexy glamour with such tantalizing tidbits as "she sleeps in the nude," or "she loves champagne." Both had been married as teenagers before breaking into the film industry, and during the height of their celebrity, both were romantically linked with older, sophisticated men.

One of Marilyn's most faithful boosters and friends was columnist Sidney Skolsky.

Marilyn was the first—and perhaps only—actress to match the sheer impact of the legendary Jean Harlow.

As Marilyn's popularity soared, the Harlow comparison faded, though the spectre of Jean Harlow haunted Marilyn in other ways. During the mid-1950s, columnist Sidney Skolsky, who had befriended Marilyn during her years as a starlet, wanted her to star in a biopic (biographical movie) of Harlow's life. Though interested, Marilyn was disappointed in the sensationalism of the script offered her by Twentieth Century-Fox. After reading it, she prophetically told her agent and friends, "I hope they don't do that to me after I'm gone." Skolsky continued to campaign for a Harlow biography starring Marilyn Monroe until the year Marilyn died. According to the columnist, "On the Sunday they found Marilyn dead, I had an appointment with her for that afternoon at four to work on *The Jean Harlow Story*." (A pair of mediocre Harlow biopics did finally appear in 1965, one starring Carol Lynley, the other featuring Carroli Baker.)

Aside from making her a full-fledged star who invited comparisons with a legend of Hollywood's past, *Niagara* was important to Marilyn on a more personal level as well. During the shooting of the film in the summer of 1952, Joe DiMaggio began to seriously court Marilyn Monroe. Earlier that spring, a mutual acquaintance of Marilyn and Joe's had arranged for them to meet at DiMaggio's request. The legendary ballplayer—retired since 1951—had seen a publicity photograph of Marilyn with Chicago White Sox players Joe Dobson and Gus Zernial, and he had tracked her down from there.

Marilyn was reluctant to meet DiMaggio. She didn't follow baseball and was not attracted to sports figures. She expected DiMaggio to be wearing flashy clothes and to have slicked-back hair. "I had thought I was going to meet a loud, sporty fellow," she said later. "Instead I found myself smiling at a reserved gentleman in a gray suit, with a gray tie and a sprinkle of gray in his hair. There were a few blue polka dots in his tie. If I hadn't been told he was some sort of ballplayer, I would have guessed he was either a steel magnate or a congressman."

Two of the many faces of Marilyn Monroe.
Left: *Swinging for the fences with Gus Zernial (left) and Joe Dobson, in the newspaper photo that piqued the interest of Joe DiMaggio.*
Above: *Turning on the glamour.*

One of DiMaggio's chief rivals was Charlie McCarthy, who romanced Marilyn in late 1952.

At LaGuardia Airport in the summer of 1952, Marilyn gives New York City a big hello.

Though DiMaggio had made a good first impression, Marilyn hesitated to go out with him again. She reportedly told the man who had introduced them, "He struck out." The soft-spoken DiMaggio was smitten, however, and he phoned Marilyn repeatedly. His persistence eventually paid off, and despite their differences, the unlikely couple began dating.

Their relationship was fraught with problems almost from the beginning, mostly stemming from the public nature of Marilyn's career. A shy man, DiMaggio shunned publicity and the press, while Marilyn's career thrived on it. DiMaggio disliked the hustle and limelight of Hollywood; Marilyn was inextricably caught up in it. DiMaggio protected Marilyn to some degree from the brutal side of Hollywood: the steel-hearted studio executives, the phony hangers-on, the snide remarks in the press about her acting abilities. He could not understand her devotion to such a distasteful business. As a further annoyance, DiMaggio and Natasha Lytess had a mutual dislike and distrust for each other. Lytess thought Marilyn could do better than a former baseball player, while DiMaggio resented Lytess's control over Marilyn. As Marilyn and Joe grew closer, the relationship between the actress and her coach became less personal and more professional.

Complicating the issue was the change in Marilyn's star status from the time of the couple's initial meeting through their serious courtship. At the beginning of their romance, Marilyn was still appearing in minor or secondary roles at Fox. In the aftermath of the nude calendar story and throughout the production of *Niagara*, the publicity surrounding Hollywood's hottest starlet rapidly increased. Marilyn began to participate in more and more promotional functions—just the sort of events DiMaggio shunned. Bandleader Ray Anthony, for example, introduced a song called "Marilyn," written by Ervin Drake and Jimmy Shirl. The song was presented to Marilyn by Mickey Rooney and Anthony at a party at Anthony's home. In true Hollywood style, Marilyn arrived at the poolside party in a helicopter. She was wearing the provocative red dress she had worn in *Niagara*. More the impetus for a publicity stunt rather than an exciting, new pop song, "Marilyn" never made the top ten. With such lyrics as "No gal, I believe, beginning with Eve, could weave a fascination like my Ma-ri-lyn," the tune was doomed to novelty status.

*Bandleader Ray Anthony hosted a
party for Marilyn in 1952, on the occasion of
"Marilyn," a new song about her. In the classic
Hollywood tradition of splashy entrances, Marilyn
arrived in a helicopter. Anthony's fondness for
blondes was apparently the real thing, for he later
married actress Mamie Van Doren.*

A month later, Marilyn was the Grand Marshal for the parade for the 1952 Miss America pageant. During the festivities, she was asked to pose with several women from the armed services. The low-cut summer dress she was wearing caught the attention of a photographer, who stood on a chair to better capture the outfit's full effect. Upon seeing the photo, an Army information officer ordered it killed because he did not want to give the parents of potential recruits the "wrong impression" about Army life. Information about the suppression of the photo was leaked to the press and then turned into front-page news. When asked her opinion of the situation for a story titled "Marilyn Wounded by Army Blushoff," Marilyn replied in her tongue-in-cheek manner, "I am very surprised and very hurt. I wasn't aware of any objectionable décolletage on my part. I'd noticed people looking at me all day, but I thought they were admiring my Grand Marshal's badge!"

In September 1952, Marilyn was Grand Marshal of the Miss America parade.

Not surprisingly, the dress caught the fancy of photographers, one of whom climbed onto a chair to snap Marilyn and female military personnel.

Later during the festivities, she changed into a more comfortable summer dress and chatted with Miss Indiana.

The relentless emphasis by reporters and press agents on Marilyn's physical attributes became a sore point with DiMaggio as the romance progressed. Many assume that his quiet dignity and conservative demeanor made it difficult for him to accept any display or discussion of Marilyn's sexuality or famous figure. It is possible that DiMaggio was just as angered by the press's condescending and often snide attitude toward Marilyn. As a popular, even beloved, celebrity himself, DiMaggio had had many personal encounters with the press and an adoring public. But the attention given him since the start of his own memorable career had been of a completely different nature than the attention paid to Marilyn. In the end, DiMaggio's unhappiness with the press's treatment of Marilyn did nothing to alter the tone of the coverage. In fact, after the release of *Niagara*, the number of stories revolving around Marilyn's sexuality both on and off the screen steadily increased.

"Leg art" photo sessions were a never-ending part of Marilyn's career, and one that she worked at with enthusiasm and good humor.

Throughout her career, Marilyn was the stuff of dreams to magazine editors. She was indeed "MMmmmm!"

As her fame escalated in the early 1950s, Marilyn's image adorned the covers of magazines of many sorts, including digest-size "men's" magazines of the type pictured here.

Increased press coverage brought headaches, but also contributed to an improvement in Marilyn's status at Twentieth Century-Fox throughout the production of *Niagara*. On June 1, 1952, Fox gave Marilyn a surprise birthday present—the news that she would star as Lorelei Lee in the film version of *Gentlemen Prefer Blondes*. A smash success on the Broadway stage, *Gentlemen Prefer Blondes* had been running for over two years with Carol Channing starring as the vivacious Lorelei. Hollywood clamored for several months to secure the film rights to the hit musical. Columbia negotiated for the property as a vehicle for their blonde comedy star, Judy Holliday, while Fox originally wanted it for Betty Grable. Grable campaigned heavily for the part, realizing the importance of the role to her faltering career. The actress with the million-dollar legs had been Fox's top box-office draw during Marilyn's unsuccessful tenure at the studio in the late 1940s—an era when many a blonde starlet was molded in Grable's image. Ironically, by 1952, Marilyn's star was fast eclipsing Grable's.

Gentlemen Prefer Blondes began production in November 1952. Reportedly, costar Jane Russell received between $100,000 and $200,000 for her appearance, while Marilyn was under contract for $1,500 per week. She earned about $18,000 for her work in the picture, while Grable might have cost Fox as much as $150,000. Aware that she was being taken advantage of, Marilyn insisted on her own dressing room. As she told the Fox executives, "I *am* the blonde, and it is *Gentlemen Prefer Blondes*."

Marilyn and Jane Russell developed a strong, friendly relationship during the shooting of the film, much to the disappointment of the popular press, which was eager to report a feud between the two sex symbols. But *Gentlemen Prefer Blondes* did have some genuine problems. It was during the production of this film that Marilyn's tendency to show up late to the set greatly intensified. Her makeup man, Whitey Snyder, realized that Marilyn was actually terrified to appear in front of the cameras and had to work up her nerve to begin the day's shooting. Though she often arrived at the studio an hour before Russell, Marilyn could not bring herself to go out onto the set. Director Howard Hawks—not known for tolerating the frailties of actors—became upset at Marilyn's tardiness, which brought a great deal of tension to the production. Snyder confided his suspicions about Marilyn to Jane Russell, who made it a point to stop by Marilyn's dressing room every morning and walk with the frightened young star onto the set. Russell not only understood Marilyn's insecurities but also the harsh, insensitive nature of the film industry; the savvy actress seemed to sense that Marilyn was unable to withstand the cruelties of the business.

The plum role of Lorelei Lee in Gentlemen Prefer Blondes *confirmed and increased the level of Marilyn's stardom.*

Marilyn and Jane Russell—a formidable presence in her
own right—made a congenial team, on screen and off.
Russell was patient with Marilyn's nervousness and
lateness, and went out of her way to comfort the less
experienced actress.

Though Marilyn may have incurred Hawks's wrath with her tardiness, he could not fault her for lack of dedication. Marilyn impressed many among the cast and crew with her willingness to work hard. She continued to rehearse long after others had tired, and she requested retakes of scenes she felt were not up to par. Marilyn realized that she had been given a choice role in a highly publicized film—a part that other, more respected stars had coveted. She knew that this was her chance for critical acclaim, her chance to garner some respect in the industry.

Marilyn's performance as Lorelei was a deftly comic one that was perfectly complemented by the more jaundiced nature of Dorothy, the character played by Russell.

Marilyn would eventually become notorious for causing difficulties during the production of her films, yet she managed to work with some of Hollywood's legendary directors in her brief career—actually working with some of them twice. Howard Hawks, for example, had directed Marilyn before, in *Monkey Business*. Hawks always maintained that "A great personality illuminates the screen," feeling that a successful end product made any on-set difficulties irrelevant. During his lengthy career, the veteran director galvanized movie screens with strong films highlighted by excellent performances from John Wayne, Cary Grant, Humphrey Bogart, Katharine Hepburn, John Barrymore, Carole Lombard, and Lauren Bacall. The Hawks name is most often linked with that level of larger-than-life screen actor—a class of performer that most surely includes Marilyn Monroe.

At first glance, Lorelei appears to be completely bubbleheaded, but Marilyn's subtle interpretation of the role reveals the quick and determined mind that hides behind Lorelei's guileless exterior.

Gentlemen Prefer Blondes represents a curious combination of some of Hawks's key themes and characteristics common to his movies. Best known for action films, Hawks tended to stress masculine values. His storylines often focus on a pair of tough male professionals, who seem to be opposite in type. Rather than a source of friction, however, their opposition is presented as complementary. In *Blondes*, Marilyn and Jane Russell have assumed the usually male roles of opposite yet complementary types: Lorelei is blonde while Jane's character, Dorothy, is brunette; Lorelei wants to marry for money, while Dorothy intends to marry for love; Lorelei is presented as the epitome of the dumb blonde while Dorothy is clever and resourceful. Despite their extreme differences, the two characters not only perform together on the stage but also join forces to resolve problems in the area of romance. By focusing on the point of view of Lorelei and Dorothy as they survey the male population for suitable husbands or companions, *Blondes* seems to parody those films in which predatory male characters continually eye women as objects of desire. Nowhere is this more evident than in the production number "Ain't There Anyone Here for Love," in which Dorothy scrutinizes the scantily clad men of the U.S. Olympic team as they flex their muscles in front of her.

Marilyn's participation in print ads not only kept her face and name before the public, but was a clever way to boost the box-office receipts of particular films.

Gentlemen Prefer Blondes *provided a lively showcase for the singing and dancing of the beautiful costars.*

Original ad art for Gentlemen Prefer Blondes. *The prominence of Howard Hawks's name suggests his box-office clout.*

The film's domination by the two female characters is reinforced by the absence of any strong, dashing leading men. The odd assortment of male figures who flock around Dorothy and Lorelei include a henpecked elderly millionaire, played by jowly Charles Coburn; a little boy with a roving eye, played by young George Winslow; a dull-looking private detective, played by character actor Elliott Reid; and the weak-willed son of a socially prominent family, played by bespectacled Tommy Noonan. From the film's opening moments to its final shot, Marilyn and Jane Russell simply blow their male counterparts off the screen.

Marilyn and Jane are ogled by the male cast members of Gentlemen Prefer Blondes *(from top), Charles Coburn, Elliott Reid, Tommy Noonan, and George Winslow.*

Charles Coburn's on-screen attentions to his leading ladies—particularly Marilyn—are lecherously funny.

Despite the picture's novel interpretation of the battle of the sexes, *Gentlemen Prefer Blondes* has been attacked by contemporary critics for such obviously masculine touches as the set decor in the "Diamonds Are a Girl's Best Friend" number, in which female bodies are lashed to chandeliers as part of their support structure. Elsewhere, such dated lines as "I can be smart when it's important, but most men don't like it," made even Marilyn cringe when she read them at the time.

Lively and good-humored, *Gentlemen Prefer Blondes* is widely acknowledged as one of Marilyn's best films. It is a credit to the professionalism of both Marilyn and Howard Hawks that none of the friction between them interfered with the results on the screen. Marilyn's hard work paid off in the form of several well-executed, dynamic production numbers in which both she and Jane Russell—neither of whom were renowned for their singing and dancing abilities—sparkled. Marilyn's show-stopping "Diamonds Are a Girl's Best Friend" would become her signature song, highlighting her beauty and grace and also capturing the youthful actress at a high point in her career. In retrospect, the number signifies that moment in time when Marilyn was in control of her life and her destiny—a moment as fleeting as it was joyful.

Reviews of *Gentlemen Prefer Blondes* were generally favorable, though many critics still focused on Marilyn's physical attributes rather than on her performance. Those few who did discuss her talents debated among themselves exactly how well she could sing or dance. According to *Time* magazine, Darryl F. Zanuck anticipated accusations that the pleasing singing voice of Lorelei Lee was not Marilyn's, so he signed an affidavit affirming that the voice on the soundtrack was indeed hers.

The show-stopping "Diamonds Are a Girl's Best Friend" number is the dazzling highlight of Gentlemen Prefer Blondes. *The exuberant song will forever be identified with Marilyn.*

Little pets get big baguettes. Marilyn shows off a few of Lorelei's best friends.

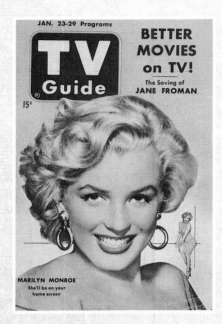

So great was Marilyn's popularity in 1953 that she was featured on the cover of TV Guide *some eight months in advance of her television debut.*

In early 1953, Marilyn was honored with Redbook *magazine's Best Young Box Office Personality award. Celebrity guests at the presentation included (from left) Dean Martin, Leslie Caron, and Jerry Lewis.*

If the critics remained divided about Marilyn, the public had long since made up its mind that Marilyn Monroe was a bona fide star. Marilyn received a number of awards shortly after the production of *Gentlemen Prefer Blondes* that not only signified her popularity with the public but also put her in the spotlight in more ways than one.

In the spring of 1953, *Redbook,* a woman's magazine that had been generally favorable to Marilyn, honored her with its Best Young Box Office Personality award. She had also won *Look* magazine's award for Most Promising Female Newcomer of 1952. However, these tributes to her stardom were totally eclipsed by the circumstances surrounding an award given Marilyn by *Photoplay* movie magazine in March 1953. *Photoplay* dubbed Marilyn the "Fastest Rising Star of 1952" and presented her with a plaque during a prestigious awards ceremony. For the occasion, Marilyn wore one of the dresses designed by Billy Travilla for *Gentlemen Prefer Blondes*. The form-fitting gold lamé gown was so tight that Marilyn had to be sewn into it. As she walked away from the podium after receiving her award, the audience hooted and screamed at the sight of her voluptuous body swaying across the stage. Some accounts of the evening's events report that comedian Jerry Lewis leaped up on his table and whistled wildly.

Surprisingly, the press seemed more aghast at Marilyn's presumptuousness for wearing such a costume than they were at the audience's uncivilized behavior. *Time* magazine called for Hollywood to "go easier on the sex angle" after reporting on the affair, while former glamour queen Joan Crawford lambasted Marilyn in Bob Thomas's syndicated column. Crawford told Thomas that the sight of Marilyn caused "those of us in the industry" to shudder (as though Marilyn was somehow not in the industry), and went on to say, "She should be told that the public likes provocative female personalities; but it also likes to know that underneath it all, the actresses are ladies."

Marilyn was tremendously hurt by Crawford's haughty comments and used her ally in the press, Louella Parsons, to fight back. Parsons quoted Marilyn as saying: ". . . Why should [Crawford] select me to blast? She is a great star. I'm just starting. And then, when the first hurt began to die down, I told myself she must have spoken to Mr. Thomas impulsively, without thinking. . . ."

Marilyn suffered some bad publicity
after wearing this gold lamé gown to the
March 1953 Photoplay *awards.*
The dress was so tight that
Marilyn had to be sewn into it,
and her appearance caused a sensation at the ceremony.
Marilyn used her allies in the press to publicly
defend herself against critical comments.

The publicity surrounding Marilyn was once again focused on her sexuality at the expense of her identity as a person and as an actress. Though her films revolved to a large extent around that sexuality, her movie roles represented a much more complex use of the sexual aspect of her image. Her publicity and studio promotion tended to extract her sexuality and emphasize it, resulting in condescending remarks by critics about her acting abilties, criticisms of her behavior by women's groups, and snickering comments by the press about her figure. Both Marilyn and companion Joe DiMaggio grew increasingly upset at the inability of the press and public to separate her highly artificial image from her off-screen life.

A reflective moment, 1953.

During this period of Marilyn's rapidly rising stardom, it is easy to trace her life and career through a series of major publicity events. The negative reaction to the *Photoplay* ceremony in the spring of 1953 soon gave way to more positive publicity surrounding the imprinting of her handprints and footprints in the forecourt of Grauman's Chinese Theater in June of that same year. Thanks to the box-office success of *Gentlemen Prefer Blondes*, Marilyn and Jane Russell were asked to appear together to place their prints and signatures in the cement. A hallowed tradition in Hollywood, the honor offered visual proof of an actor's stardom. In her tongue-in-cheek manner, Marilyn suggested that if these prints were supposed to signify a performer's screen image, then Russell should lean forward so her bust would be imprinted in the cement while she should simply sit in it! She also suggested that a diamond chip be used to dot the "i" in Marilyn, but officials used a rhinestone instead. Predictably, a star-struck thief soon pried the stone from its place.

Joe DiMaggio's courtship of Marilyn fascinated the world. Here, the couple share a quiet moment in Banff, Canada, in 1953.

Like many children who grew up near Hollywood, young Norma Jeane was drawn to the famed cement forecourt of Grauman's Chinese Theater. On June 26, 1953, Marilyn and Jane Russell left their prints and signatures in wet cement, joining the ranks of Hollywood's greatest stars.

How to Marry a Millionaire, Marilyn's next film, became the first comedy to be released in CinemaScope. If there was some trepidation that a comedy would not be able to make adequate use of the new widescreen process, then Twentieth Century-Fox hedged its bets by featuring three top blonde stars in the main roles. Though supposedly based on a non-fiction best-seller by Doris Lilly, Fox executives discarded just about everything but the title and based the screenplay on a handful of plays that the studio owned. Lauren Bacall and Betty Grable costarred with Marilyn in the film, with William Powell, Rory Calhoun, David Wayne, and Cameron Mitchell rounding out the male half of the cast.

How to Marry a Millionaire was directed by Jean Negulesco and scripted by the well-respected Nunnally Johnson. Though several unkind remarks about Marilyn would later be attributed to Johnson, she got along quite well with Negulesco, who had a reputation in the industry as a woman's director. During the production of the film, the artist-turned-director painted an oil portrait of his timid star and lent her several books, which he and Marilyn discussed at length. However, in recountings of the production of this particular film, it is not how well Marilyn got along with her director that is best remembered but how well she got along with her female costars.

Marilyn is joined by director Jean Negulesco and costar Betty Grable on the set of How to Marry a Millionaire. *Though the press anticipated that sparks would fly between Grable and the younger Marilyn . . .*

. . . the two stars got along well. Grable was well aware that Fox was easing her out in favor of Marilyn, but she never treated Marilyn with anything but kindness.

Lauren Bacall completed
the female part of the picture's cast.
Playing ambitious women determined to marry rich men,
the three stars enjoyed a splendid showcase for their talents.

Longtime Hollywood star William Powell and the widescreen CinemaScope process were among the many selling points of How to Marry a Millionaire.

Just as the entertainment press had eagerly anticipated a feud between Marilyn and Jane Russell during *Gentlemen Prefer Blondes,* so they were hoping for some sparks to fly between Marilyn and Betty Grable on the set of *Millionaire.* Considering the manner in which Marilyn's path had fatefully crossed Grable's during their careers, tension between the two stars would have come as no surprise. Yet, Grable was unselfishly kind to Marilyn and harbored no resentment toward the new blonde on the Fox lot. Grable had defended Marilyn earlier that year over the controversy concerning her dress at the *Photoplay* awards, telling reporters that she was "a shot in the arm for Hollywood." Later, in front of several people on the set, Grable reportedly told Marilyn, "Honey, I've had it. Go get yours. It's your turn now." Undoubtedly, Grable did feel she was being pushed aside, but she never blamed Marilyn. Instead, she directed her anger at Zanuck and Twentieth Century-Fox; on July 1, 1953, she stormed into Zanuck's office and tore up her contract.

Marilyn reciprocated Grable's kindness in small ways, despite the problems she often had coping with shyness and communicating with some of her peers. For instance, when Grable went home to care for one of her children who had become ill, Marilyn was the only person who called to inquire about the boy's condition. After Grable left Fox, Marilyn inherited her dressing room, which was located in the Star Building on the Fox lot. Photographers wanted Marilyn to pose in front of the dressing room while Grable's name was still on it to suggest that Marilyn had succeeded her at Fox. She refused; she wanted no part of making Betty Grable feel as though she were finished.

Pola, the desperately nearsighted character played by Marilyn, declares, "Men aren't attentive to girls who wear glasses." Pola's insistence on leaving her glasses in her handbag provided Marilyn with opportunities to demonstrate her flair for physical comedy.

Lauren Bacall found it more difficult to warm up to Marilyn than Grable had, perhaps because of Marilyn's continual tardiness on the set, her constant need for approval from Natasha Lytess, and her request for incessant retakes—behavior Bacall considered unprofessional. Marilyn's insecurities about her acting abilities and her sensitivity to the criticism of others made working in front of a movie camera much more difficult for her than modeling for a still camera had ever been. Her anxieties intensified as her roles became larger and her films more important, resulting in her need to bolster her confidence before appearing on the set. Most often, her insecurities took several hours to overcome. She was consistently late to the set, which caused hard feelings because the rest of the cast had to wait for her, often for several hours. Marilyn needed the approval of Lytess for each scene and looked directly at her at the end of each take; if Lytess shook her head disapprovingly, Marilyn requested a retake. The timid star tended to become more secure and give a better performance with each additional take, while her costars often lost their edge and spontaneity as the number of retakes increased. But despite any hardships Marilyn put the cast through during the production of *Millionaire*, Bacall never spoke harshly of her costar. The gracious actress later wrote in her autobiography: "A scene often went to 15 or more takes . . . not easy, often irritating. And yet I didn't dislike Marilyn. She had no meanness in her—no bitchery. . . . There was something sad about her—wanting to reach out—afraid to trust—uncomfortable. She made no effort for others and yet she was nice."

How to Marry a Millionaire *captures many of the key elements of Marilyn's image: glamour, sex appeal, and an agreeable touch of self-spoofery.*

Lauren Bacall, a disciplined actress and a full-fledged Hollywood star by the time she was 20, was less tolerant than Betty Grable of Marilyn's on-set anxiety. Yet Bacall was touched by Marilyn's vulnerability.

Marilyn was joined at the premiere of How to Marry a Millionaire *by Lauren Bacall and Bacall's husband, Humphrey Bogart.*

Besides Marilyn, guests at a premiere party given by Jean Negulesco included (from left) Rock Hudson, Terry Moore, and Robert Mitchum.

Marilyn's role in *Millionaire* showcased her talents as a comedienne, which many biographers and industry personnel have suggested was her true calling. As Pola Debevoise, Marilyn played a nearsighted department store model who never wears her glasses because, as Pola soberly notes, "Men aren't attentive to girls who wear glasses." Pola's poor eyesight causes her to walk into walls, trip across the floor, and stumble on stairs. The sight of such a beautiful, voluptuous star as Marilyn Monroe blundering gracelessly into walls heightened the comic effect.

Marilyn's ability to perform physical stunts so adroitly was probably the result of her keen awareness of her body. She had always used her physical attributes to suggest aspects of her film characters; she had a knowledge and understanding of anatomy that other actresses did not possess. She had studied human bone and muscle structure to help accentuate her physical presence, and coworkers have often testified how she practiced walking, gesturing, and even moving her facial muscles in front of a mirror. Her work began to pay off in *How to Marry a Millionaire*. Though generally regarded as lightweight fare, the picture was a critical and popular success. Marilyn was singled out in the majority of film reviews for her comic performance, though, once again, critics were reluctant to admit that she was truly talented.

Shortly after the release of *Millionaire*, an unusual criticism of Marilyn appeared in East Germany's *Berliner Illustrierte*. A front-page article in the communist newspaper blamed the young star for many of the political ills plaguing America. The paper claimed that her function was to make the American people forget about the Korean War and the high cost of living. The paper pontificated: "During the premiere of [*How to Marry a Millionaire*] in New York, fans literally tore her clothing from her body and hardly noticed that at the same time [Senator Joseph] McCarthy was violating the great democratic traditions of the American people." The article is not only amusing in its dogmatic interpretation of Marilyn's impact on our country, but also indicates that her fame extended worldwide.

How to Marry a Millionaire *was a box-office hit.*
Its success not only established Marilyn as the most
important actress on the Fox lot,
but as a movie star
with international appeal and influence.

Marilyn was featured in three consecutive box-office hits in 1953, a streak of good fortune that made her the hottest screen star of that year. Reviews of these films often singled her out for acclaim or attention, and she continued to receive vast quantities of fan mail each week. Her romance with American baseball hero Joe DiMaggio kept her name in the news on a regular basis. Thus, it remains a mystery to biographers and fans why Twentieth Century-Fox did not take advantage of Marilyn's celebrity to showcase her image and talents in a quality production. Instead, the studio assigned her to *River of No Return*, an action-oriented western that made wiser use of its CinemaScope format than it did of Marilyn's talent and image. This lack of foresight lends credence to Marilyn's contention that studio head Darryl F. Zanuck had little interest in her career as a serious actress.

Marilyn joined director Otto Preminger and costar Robert Mitchum in Canada to make River of No Return.

Though Marilyn was pleased to have been teamed with the formidable Mitchum, she remained unimpressed with the quality of the completed film.

River of No Return was directed on location in Canada by Otto Preminger. Marilyn starred as Kay Weston, a struggling saloon singer earning a meager wage in a backwoods mining camp. Together with rugged homesteader Robert Mitchum and his young son, played by Tommy Rettig, she embarks on a journey by raft down the legendary River of No Return—a trip made perilous by the presence of Indians, thieves, and white-water rapids.

The production of the film was pretty perilous, too, thanks to hard-nosed Otto Preminger, who fought with Marilyn and Natasha Lytess during most of the shoot. Marilyn's dependence on Natasha's coaching infuriated Preminger, who objected to someone else "directing" the star of his film. The Austrian-born actor-director actually banned Lytess from the set at one point, supposedly for upsetting little Tommy Rettig so badly that he could not remember his lines. Marilyn responded by phoning Zanuck to request that Lytess be reinstated on the condition that she promise not to speak to cast members other than Marilyn; Zanuck sided with Marilyn and telegraphed Preminger to let the repentent coach back on the set.

Marilyn injured her left ankle during the shoot of River of No Return; *as Joe DiMaggio rushed to the location, male crew members obligingly played taxi.*

Other problems plagued the production of the film as well, including cost overruns when the shoot fell behind schedule. Robert Mitchum tagged the film "Picture of No Return," alluding to its potential as a box-office disaster. Preminger's insistence that the cast perform many of their own stunts resulted in several accidents. In one incident, Marilyn and Mitchum were riding the raft when it became stuck on the rocks in the middle of the river. Just as the raft was about to turn over, a couple of stuntmen reached the two stars by lifeboat, averting disaster. Some time later, Marilyn injured her left ankle, though the severity of the injury is debated among those who knew her. Doctors did put a plaster cast on her leg, but actress Shelley Winters—a friend of Marilyn's who was working on another film nearby—claims in her autobiography that Marilyn faked the severity of the sprain so that Preminger would treat her more sympathetically.

DiMaggio rushed to the set with his own doctor after hearing of the injury and spent several days with Marilyn while she recuperated. The couple continued to dodge questions from reporters about wedding plans, though it was obvious that the two celebrities were romantically involved. Whether Preminger was moved by Marilyn's injury or by the need to complete the film, he did treat her with more respect for the rest of the shoot. Between Joe's presence on the set and the change in Preminger's attitude, she managed to finish the film without further incident.

Though *River of No Return* was not the unmitigated disaster humorously predicted by Mitchum, the film was not a box-office sensation and received only lukewarm reviews. Marilyn herself was much harsher in her opinion of the film than any critic had been, referring to *River* as "a Z cowboy movie in which the acting finishes third to the scenery and CinemaScope."

Though no classic, River of No Return
did at least give Marilyn the chance to sing.

*Tommy Rettig, Marilyn, and Mitchum
negotiate the treacherous river by raft. During
the filming of another scene, Marilyn and
Mitchum were in momentary peril when the
raft nearly turned over in the water.*

*The movie's title tune is pleasant,
but even Marilyn was unable to make much of songs such as
"I'm Going to File My Claim" and
"Down in the Meadow."*

Broken Arrow *and other "adult westerns"*
of the early 1950s gave the genre new life, and it was
almost inevitable that Marilyn would appear in one.
Unfortunately, River of No Return
turned out to be tepid stuff.

Marilyn made her TV guest-star debut in September 1953, on The Jack Benny Program. She sang "Bye Bye Baby" . . .

. . . and exchanged some clever banter with Benny, seen here with indispensable sidekick Eddie "Rochester" Anderson.

After the unsatisfying experience of *River of No Return*, Marilyn began to worry about the quality of the films she would be assigned in the future. Seeking control over future roles as well as a better salary, she tried to renegotiate her contract in the fall of 1953. Zanuck refused. Marilyn then requested a role in an upcoming drama titled *The Egyptian*. Instead, the studio assigned her to a lightweight B-musical with the tentative title *The Girl in Pink Tights* (also known as *Pink Tights*). Marilyn's costar on this fluffy musical comedy was to be Frank Sinatra, who would receive $5000 per week while working on the Fox lot. Though Marilyn was indisputably the bigger star at the time, she was still earning only $1500 per week.

Tempers flared when Marilyn demanded a copy of the script to read before she would agree to appear step before the cameras. Zanuck refused, standing firm in his belief that Marilyn was under contract and should simply do as she was told. The studio ordered her to report for the first day of shooting on December 15, 1953. This time, Marilyn refused, and Twentieth Century-Fox suspended her. According to some accounts, the studio relented at one point in the feud and sent her a copy of the script. When Marilyn discovered that the story was a trite one revolving around a schoolteacher turned saloon dancer, she notified Fox that her participation in *The Girl in Pink Tights* was out of the question. The studio threatened to dismiss her, spreading rumors that a dynamic blonde dancer named Sheree North was being groomed to replace her. Apparently unfazed, Marilyn responded by marrying Joe DiMaggio on January 14, 1954.

In 1953, the premiere issue of Playboy featured Marilyn on the cover, and one of her calendar nudes inside.

Reportedly, DiMaggio had asked Marilyn to marry him several times, but she had turned him down. Rumors had been flying for several months, speculating on when the couple involved in the storybook romance would finally take the plunge. Though others have claimed in the recent past to have dated Marilyn during her courtship with DiMaggio, no solid proof exists that she was serious about anyone except the famous Yankee Clipper. DiMaggio had always tried to protect Marilyn from the machinations of the studio executives; finally, during this battle of wills between Marilyn and Twentieth Century-Fox, he succeeded in pulling her away from their iron grip.

Marilyn garnered a lot of public and media support as a result of her marriage to an American idol. A few days after the wedding, Fox relented and told Marilyn all would be forgiven if she came back to work. A truce was finally worked out in which Marilyn's salary was adjusted and *The Girl in Pink Tights* permanently shelved.

Marilyn had promised Fox publicist Harry Brand that if she and DiMaggio decided to marry, he would be the first to know. True to her word, she called him on the morning of January 14. Brand, in turn, notified everyone else, including all the news services. The hallways of the courthouse in San Francisco, where the two said their vows, were jammed with photographers and reporters. A crowd of over 500 quickly gathered outside, trying to catch a glimpse of the fairy-tale couple. If DiMaggio had thought he could shield their private life from the watchful eye of the public and press, he was sadly mistaken.

On January 14, 1954, Marilyn and Joe DiMaggio were married. Public interest was tremendous and unremitting . . .

. . . as DiMaggio discovered from the outset, when a crush of reporters blocked the courthouse door following the ceremony.

Newsmen and thousands of fans met the honeymooners at Tokyo International Airport.

After a few days in Palm Springs, the DiMaggios left for Japan on their honeymoon. Joe had planned to combine their trip with some baseball business with partner Frank "Lefty" O'Doul. At Tokyo's International Airport, the massed fans, photographers, and reporters were so manic in their enthusiasm for Marilyn and Joe that the couple had to scramble back into their airplane. The honeymooners managed to escape a short time later through the baggage hatch. Marilyn was the number-one foreign box-office draw in Japan at that time, and fans pushed each other into hotel pools, broke plate glass windows, and jammed themselves into revolving doors in frantic efforts to see "the Honorable Buttocks-Swinging Actress," as she was referred to by the Japanese media. If DiMaggio was unhappy at the constant barrage of attention aimed his way, he must have been livid at the suggestive questions the Japanese press hurled at Marilyn during a press conference. One reporter asked her opinion of the Kinsey report on female sexuality, and a photographer ungraciously inquired if she slept in the nude. Another illustrious member of the news media wanted to know if she wore underwear.

More people awaited Marilyn and Joe at the Imperial Hotel, where the scene quickly became a bedlam. Photographers broke through the police lines, and the couple was mobbed by Japanese schoolgirls who had waited for more than three hours.

Frantic fans and rude reporters aside, Marilyn spent much of her time in Japan relaxing. At a cocktail party in Tokyo, a high-ranking American Army officer asked Marilyn if she would consider entertaining the troops stationed in Korea. Marilyn was thrilled at the request, though DiMaggio was concerned about the potential danger involved. The new bride decided in favor of Uncle Sam and interrupted her honeymoon to be airlifted by helicopter to Korea. Though some versions of this story suggest that Marilyn left for Korea over DiMaggio's serious objections, other accounts indicate that he merely voiced disapproval over her decision. Whatever the case, Marilyn's side trip did become a point of contention between the newlyweds.

Marilyn left Japan on February 16 for a side trip to Korea, where she entertained American troops.

Things got worse at a press conference, where reporters asked questions that were at once asinine and rude. As always, Marilyn kept smiling, but DiMaggio's patience was sorely tried.

Marilyn later recalled this trip as one of the highlights of her life. The pleasure that was given and received is evident here.

Marilyn would say more than once in her life that the adulation she felt in Korea by the servicemen—a group of fans who had helped make her a star—was the high point of her career. As she performed before thousands of troops in bitter cold temperatures, wearing only a scanty, plum-colored dress, she acknowledged her debt to them as they warmed her with their unconditional adoration. She sang "Diamonds Are a Girl's Best Friend," "Bye, Bye Baby," and "Do It Again," interrupting her performance to crack jokes with the soldiers about their fondness for sweater girls. "You fellas are always whistling at sweater girls," she teased. "Well, take away their sweaters and what have you got?"

Marilyn returned to Japan from her exhausting four-day trip with a 104-degree temperature and a slight case of pneumonia. DiMaggio nursed her back to health before the couple continued their honeymoon, touring some of Japan's smaller villages. Like the eye of a hurricane, this peaceful interlude lulled the couple into thinking the worst of the storm had passed.

Marilyn with the troupe that accompanied her to Korea.

Marilyn put on her traveling clothes for a first-hand impression of American armor. At the time, a United Press caption described the tank's crew as the "most-envied" in Korea.

*The temperatures in Korea were bitter cold during the
four days Marilyn performed, but she said later
that she felt only the warmth of the adoring soldiers.*

*Marilyn sang her heart out in ten shows, and
thrilled and entertained more than 100,000 troops.*

Back in the States, Joe and Marilyn took up residence at his home in San Francisco, where the DiMaggio family owned and operated a restaurant on Fisherman's Wharf. City residents allowed their famous native son and his new bride to have their privacy, but tourists continually disrupted their homelife. An award from *Photoplay* magazine as Best Actress for her performances in *Gentlemen Prefer Blondes* and *How to Marry a Millionaire* prompted Marilyn's return to Hollywood, as did the starting date for her next film.

Marilyn with Donald O'Connor in There's No Business Like Show Business.

Twentieth Century-Fox persuaded Marilyn to appear in the star-studded but hopelessly dated musical *There's No Business Like Show Business* by promising her the leading role in the film version of *The Seven Year Itch*. Marilyn agreed, but her part in *Show Business* was secondary compared to the star turns of Ethel Merman and Dan Dailey. The remainder of the cast included dancers Donald O'Connor and Mitzi Gaynor as well as sob-singer Johnnie Ray. Instead of showcasing the individual talents of each of the performers, this wildly uneven musical merely emphasized their differences. Merman's brassy singing style overwhelmed those of her fellow cast members, while Ray, known for the tune "Cry" and similarly fevered pop records, appeared stiff and artificial throughout. And beside the manic tap routines of O'Connor and Gaynor, Marilyn's soft singing voice and sensual mannerisms seemed inappropriately languid.

In some scenes, the aggressive dancing of O'Connor and Mitzi Gaynor (right) nearly overwhelmed Marilyn's more subdued style.

*In her own dance numbers, though,
Marilyn dominated
the screen, and was the film's sole source of sizzle.*

Marilyn's torrid "Heat Wave" number is the eye-popping highlight of Show Business.

The film's liveliest production number was a torrid version of "Heat Wave" performed by Marilyn and a bevy of male dancers. Considered controversial at the time, the number featured Marilyn in a flamenco skirt slit all the way up the front. The bumps and grinds that were part of the choreography revealed the black leotard-bottom underneath her costume, and outraged some observers who were not accustomed to this sort of unblushing display. Reviewers added to the controversy by singling out the number as vulgar or crude. Bosley Crowther of *The New York Times* stated that Marilyn's "wriggling and squirming . . . are embarrassing to behold." *Time* magazine intoned that Marilyn "bumps and grinds as expressively as the law will allow."

Whatever the reasons for assigning Marilyn to *There's No Business Like Show Business*, Fox executives miscalculated once again in regard to her talents and image. Marilyn eventually became adamant—almost stubborn—about certain details or bits of dialogue in her films, a habit that was probably caused by years of being pushed around and ill-used by the studio.

As this image suggests,
There's No Business Like Show Business *is colorful,*
splashy . . . and trivial.
From left, Johnnie Ray, Mitzi Gaynor, Dan Dailey,
Ethel Merman, Donald O'Connor, and Marilyn.

Marilyn agreed to appear in Show Business *only after*
Fox promised her the lead in the movie version of the
hit play, The Seven Year Itch.

Marilyn at New York's Idlewild Airport, September 1954. She was in town to shoot scenes for The Seven Year Itch, *one of her best and most important films.*

As soon as *Show Business* wrapped, Marilyn was ushered immediately, without a rest, to the set of *The Seven Year Itch*. Production began in Hollywood in August of 1954 and continued in New York the following month. DiMaggio did not accompany Marilyn on her trip east. After just a few months as husband and wife, Joe and Marilyn were experiencing problems. She had collapsed three times during the production of *Show Business*, supposedly because of the tension at home, and he had visited her on the set only once. Most accounts of her life reveal that the marital discord resulted from Marilyn's career. DiMaggio became increasingly annoyed with the phoniness and artificiality of the movie industry and was futher angered by the studio's repeated efforts to imprison Marilyn in blonde bombshell roles. Despite the fact that *The Seven Year Itch* was based on a successful play by renowned playwright George Axelrod, DiMaggio saw Marilyn's part only as another in a series of sexy, dumb blonde roles.

Marilyn watches dailies during the Itch *shoot.*

DiMaggio eventually joined his wife in New York, but their relationship moved from disharmony to disaster after the shooting of one of Marilyn's most legendary scenes, the moment in which she stands above a subway grate to feel the rush of air that passes whenever a train rushes beneath her. The shot of Marilyn's white dress billowing up to reveal her shapely legs is so identified with her image that it has become a virtual icon, at once celebrating her sexuality and encapsulating her legend. The scene was shot at 52nd Street and Lexington in New York City in the middle of the night. Despite the late hour, thousands of fans showed up to catch a glimpse of Marilyn Monroe. So many flashbulbs went off each time director Billy Wilder tried to shoot a take that he made a deal with the amateur photographers and the press: If they would allow him to shoot the scene, he would ask Marilyn to pose for them.

*Director Billy Wilder
(left) sets up the famous
skirt-blowing scene.*

*Shot at 52nd Street and Lexington Avenue in New York
City, the scene delighted more than 2000 onlookers.
Costar Tom Ewell had plenty to smile about . . .*

*. . . but Joe DiMaggio watched in stony silence. The
following day, he returned to California—alone. He
and Marilyn separated less than a month later.*

Despite Marilyn's personal troubles, the business of moviemaking had to go on. In pain in November 1954, just a day before entering the hospital for gynecological surgery, Marilyn gamely posed for publicity photos.

Nothing can diminish the joy of this, the most famous of Marilyn's film scenes.

During the proceedings, DiMaggio walked onto the set, dismayed at the sight of his wife on exhibit for more than 2000 strangers. His oft-quoted remark, "What the hell's going on here?" reflects his disdain not only for the public display of Marilyn's physical charms but also for her profession, which required it. Shortly after this highly publicized event, Marilyn and Joe filed for divorce.

Just as their courtship, marriage, and honeymoon had been played out on the front pages, so the announcement of their divorce would generate a barrage of publicity and media attention. In early October, after the cast and crew returned to Hollywood, the distraught actress called director Billy Wilder and Fox publicist Harry Brand to tell them that she and Joe were divorcing. Brand released the information to the news services, and reporters descended on the DiMaggios' Beverly Hills residence en masse, staking out the house for more than two days. On October 6, Marilyn was scheduled to hold a news conference, but was too upset to say very much. As she and famed Hollywood lawyer Jerry Giesler walked out of the front door, reporters and photographers lunged forward, hurling embarrassing questions at her. Joe Hyams, then a correspondent for the *New York Herald Tribune*, was still appalled by the memory of the spectacle years later. He said he could still see "as clearly as I had seen it then, her tear-stained face as she came out of the front door, the half-a-hundred newsmen crowded in on her like animals at the kill. Only little Sidney Skolsky tried to protect her. Something about the scene and my profession of journalism sickened me."

On October 27, 1954, attorney Jerry Giesler helped Marilyn with the paperwork that made final her divorce from Joe DiMaggio.

*At a press conference three weeks earlier,
Marilyn had tearfully announced the end of her marriage.
Her heartbreak and disappointment were very real—
once again, she was alone.*

A short time later, Marilyn attempted to report to the set of *The Seven Year Itch*, which was wrapping production in the studio in Hollywood. Wilder sent her home. With a bit of understatement, he said, "She has a comedy part, and she couldn't see much comedy in life today." Marilyn had been late to the set several times before the announcement of the divorce, and the producers now feared the worst. But, surprising everyone, Marilyn jumped back into her role with total concentration. She was so engaged in her work that Wilder often got what he wanted after only one or two takes.

None of the turmoil of Marilyn's personal life ended up on the screen. *The Seven Year Itch* is considered one of Marilyn's best films, for a variety of reasons: the inspired performances by Marilyn and costar Tom Ewell, the direction by Wilder, and the script by Wilder and George Axelrod. Though Marilyn's character of the "The Girl" may appear to be just another dumb blonde, the sheer force of Marilyn's talent and personality grants the character an innocence and dimension beyond the reach of lesser actresses.

A candid shot, snapped during the filming of the final scene of The Seven Year Itch. *In the years to come, the pensive side of Marilyn's nature would become more apparent.*

The film's simple storyline revolves around the inner conflicts of Richard Sherman, a role Ewell was reprising from the Broadway production. Sherman is a very married New Yorker who daydreams and fantasizes about The Girl, a gorgeous model who has sublet the apartment above him. Sherman's wife and young son have gone away for the summer, and he seizes the opportunity to get to know The Girl. Torn between his fantasies about The Girl and his guilt over betraying his wife, Sherman eventually sees the wisdom of remaining a faithful husband.

As the object of his fantasies and desires, The Girl is, in part, a figment of Sherman's imagination. We learn little about her as an individual; she doesn't even have a name. As such, the potential exists for the character to be shallow and even unsympathetic. Yet, Marilyn's ability to combine sexuality with a childlike innocence, plus the way her natural warmth and sincerity shine through her surface glamour, elevates the character of The Girl above the level of mere sex object. The Girl is far from a buffoon; to the contrary, she is clearly at ease with her sexuality. Even when Sherman's fantasies become wild and extreme (and extremely funny), The Girl remains in control of the relationship. When she makes it clear to Sherman that romance is out of the question, she does it with wit and kindness.

The Seven Year Itch *is pure delight, and one of the*
best American film comedies of the 1950s. Here, summer
bachelor Tom Ewell meets "The Girl."

The role of The Girl was perfectly suited to Marilyn's screen image, and *The Seven Year Itch* garnered the actress some of the finest reviews of her career. With a few notable exceptions, critics focused on Marilyn's flair for comedy rather than on her shapely figure, even comparing her to the highly regarded comedienne Judy Holliday.

Aside from giving Marilyn one of the best parts of her career, *The Seven Year Itch* playfully acknowledged Marilyn's star status by incorporating elements of her own life into the character. The Girl models for men's magazines, much like Marilyn had done in her salad days. She also once posed for "an artistic picture," a tongue-in-cheek reference to Marilyn's famous calendar photo. The in-joke is carried to its extremes when a friend asks Sherman who the woman is in his kitchen, and he teasingly replies, "Marilyn Monroe." Director Billy Wilder was fond of such cinematic references to real-life Hollywood, and often incorporated amusing or cynical comments on screen legends in his films. It was an element he exploited in the next film he would direct with Marilyn, *Some Like It Hot.*

Both pages: The Seven Year Itch *is a comedy
of guilt and desire, in which the very married
Richard Sherman (Ewell) has appalling daydreams
about his curvy new neighbor.
In Sherman's comically tormented imagination, The Girl
assumes multiple guises, ranging from seductive
temptress to unscrupulous blackmailer.*

Marilyn's performance as The Girl is a subtle delight. Sexy, guileless, yet firmly in charge of her life, the character is a remarkable creation.

Marilyn studies her script between takes.

Tom Ewell, reprising his Broadway role, is pricelessly funny as Sherman. Here, a simple rendition of "Chopsticks" goes terribly awry.

In the spring of 1954, Marilyn happily accepted Photoplay magazine's "Best Actress" award.

On the set of The Seven Year Itch, *a grip
peers from behind a flat as actor Victor Moore
rehearses the extrication of The Girl's toe
from a bathtub faucet.*

On the Itch *set in 1954, Marilyn celebrates
the first anniversary of the widescreen
CinemaScope process. Joining her are Joe
DiMaggio and broadcaster/columnist Walter
Winchell (wearing hat).*

The Seven Year Itch was released in June of 1955. By that time, Marilyn was embroiled in another dispute with Fox and had formed her own production company to secure better roles. There had been a few worthwhile roles along the way, but Marilyn was generally dissatisfied with the type of parts she was assigned by Fox. She realized that the studio executives, particularly Darryl Zanuck, did not believe she had the potential to become a serious actress. Moreover, they did not *want* her to become a serious actress. She had been stereotyped as a dizzy blonde bombshell who specialized in comedies and musicals, and the studio would continue assigning her these types of roles because she had been so successful at them. In retrospect, it is difficult to understand the level of control the film studios had over the actors under contract to them; if Fox determined that it was not in their financial interest to assign Marilyn dramatic roles, then they would not do so, no matter how big a star she became.

Marilyn and Joe's relationship following their divorce was marked by warmth and friendship. On June 1, 1955, DiMaggio escorted Marilyn to the premiere of The Seven Year Itch.

A lobby card from Itch.
*The film was a major
box-office success.*

In the few years since *Niagara*, Marilyn had gone from rising star to Hollywood goddess. Her salary had increased and her acting had improved tenfold. She had become the top box-office attraction in America as well as in other parts of the world. With the increase in stature came an added pressure, which was often magnified by the turbulent events of her private life. Despite the burdens of her personal and professional lives, and despite her status as a star, Marilyn decided to leave Hollywood for New York to study acting. She was determined to become a serious, dramatic actress—with or without the studio. Though a bold move for any actor, the decision was particularly courageous for Marilyn, who battled more insecurities and personal demons in a single day than most of us will in our lifetimes.

On May 19, 1955, a 52-foot-high figure of Marilyn was
unveiled above Loew's State Theatre in New York's
Times Square to promote The Seven Year Itch. The
towering image sums up Marilyn's enormous popularity.

MARILYN, INC.

"I feel wonderful. I'm incorporated."

MARILYN MONROE, 1955

*Marilyn defied Hollywood convention
by establishing her own film production company at the end of 1954.
Suddenly, she was not only one of the world's most popular film stars,
but one of the most powerful, as well.
By 1956, secure in her beauty and confident in her developing acting skills,
Marilyn looked forward to the future.*

*9*n December 1954, shortly after the completion of *The Seven Year Itch*, Marilyn formed Marilyn Monroe Productions, Inc. with photographer Milton Greene. She had met Greene the previous year on the Fox lot when he had traveled to Hollywood to photograph her for *Look* magazine. The photographer and the former model hit it off instantly, and when they met again at a party a few days later, the two began discussing a possible partnership. Throughout 1954, Greene conferred periodically with Marilyn about his partnership proposal. During the production of *The Seven Year Itch*, negotiations began in earnest, and the company was formed a few weeks later. Marilyn Monroe Productions was established with 101 shares of stock; Marilyn controlled 51 shares, while Greene retained the remaining 50. Marilyn's function was to star in the films selected by the company, while Greene was to conduct all of the business and pay the bills. Greene, his wife Amy, his attorneys, and his accountant were all New Yorkers, an apparent reflection of the disdain Marilyn felt at this time for Hollywood and its industry personnel.

Marilyn fled Hollywood for New York after the partnership came together, leaving Twentieth Century-Fox and Darryl F. Zanuck behind. Once again, she refused to appear in a minor musical that Fox had assigned her. And once again, Fox tried to threaten Marilyn by touting Sheree North as her replacement. The studio proceeded to make the film, entitled *How to Be Very, Very Popular*, with North in Marilyn's role and Betty Grable as her costar. Fox, eager to prove that the film could be successful without Marilyn Monroe, virtually flaunted the production in her face. Nunnally Johnson, who had penned *How to Marry a Millionaire*, wrote the script, while one of Marilyn's favorite cameramen, Milton Krasner, was assigned to be the film's cinematographer. Charles Coburn and Tommy Noonan, two of her costars from *Gentlemen Prefer Blondes*, were brought in to round out the cast. But if Fox was convinced it could make a successful Marilyn Monroe film without the genuine article in the starring role, the studio was sadly mistaken. *How to Be Very, Very Popular* proved very, very unpopular at the box office and garnered only poor to mixed reviews. It remains notable mainly for a wildly exuberant dance number performed by North, and because it was the final film of Betty Grable.

*Photographer Milton Greene captured this image of
Marilyn in 1955. As Marilyn's corporate partner,
Greene proved himself as skillful a businessman as he
was a photographer. Marilyn said, "He's a genius."*

Marilyn refused other offers by Fox at this time, in particular the part of showgirl Evelyn Nesbit in *The Girl in the Red Velvet Swing*—a role that eventually went to Joan Collins. Marilyn disavowed her contract with Fox, leaving the legalities of her actions to her lawyers. After the defection of its biggest star, Fox released the following statement: "No one can handle her. No one can give her advice. She has always decided everything for herself. We're getting 200 letters a day demanding we get rid of her, but we have $2,000,000 tied up in this picture [*The Seven Year Itch*], and we're trying to protect that." By generating bad publicity about her, Fox was making sure that if it couldn't have Marilyn Monroe, then no other studio would want her. Hollywood columnists delighted in such mudslinging and printed a number of statements released through the Fox publicity department, including one that must have hit a raw nerve with Marilyn. Hedda Hopper printed this statement, supposedly from an "unnamed" Fox stockholder: "It's disgusting. She's had four or five years' training—enough to produce ten competent actresses—and she still can't act."

After turning her back on the machinations of Hollywood, Marilyn based her professional and personal activities in New York. She is seen here with Milton Greene at Idlewild Airport.

The "new" Marilyn dressed more conservatively than before, but the familiar glamour was undiminished.

Marilyn moved in with the Greenes in their Weston, Connecticut, home, far away from the machinations of Twentieth Century-Fox. In January 1955, at the height of the bad publicity generated by Fox surrounding her defection, Marilyn held a press conference in New York to formally announce the formation of Marilyn Monroe Productions, Inc. and her plans to "broaden her scope." She complained about the dumb blonde roles she had been assigned at Fox and, after some prompting by reporters, announced she would like to tackle something as challenging as Dostoyevski's *The Brothers Karamazov*. The press seized on that comment to ridicule her ambitions, snidely inquiring which of the brothers she wanted to play. She patiently replied that she would like to play Grushenka, the leading female character.

Marilyn's remarks about *The Brothers Karamazov* would be widely misquoted in print over the next few months, with the result (probably deliberate) of making Marilyn look quite foolish. Reporters questioned whether she could spell "Grushenka," let alone play the role. Over the years, the press had emphasized the sexual aspect of Marilyn's image to such a degree that they would not allow her to escape her identity as a sex symbol. When she tried, they ridiculed her.

In January 1955 Marilyn announced the formation of Marilyn Monroe Productions, Inc. It was a triumphant moment.

The New York press establishment was fascinated by Marilyn, and eagerly reported on developments surrounding her burgeoning career. But reporters still did not take her ambitions seriously—a fact that caused Marilyn no end of frustration and embarrassment.

The weeks spent at the Greenes' home proved restful for Marilyn. She could not appear in a film until her contract with Fox was negotiated to her satisfaction or officially terminated. In the meantime, she read, studied, and enjoyed the outdoors. She became close friends with Milton's wife, Amy; this warm relationship was one of the few that Marilyn enjoyed with a woman her own age. Amy Greene—a former fashion model—helped Marilyn select a new wardrobe, one more suitable to her new, more mature image, and Marilyn babysat for the Greenes' son, Josh. Since Marilyn was generating no income of her own, Milton Greene paid all of her expenses, including the rent on the Manhattan apartment Marilyn eventually occupied. Greene was dedicated to Marilyn Monroe Productions, even to the point of mortgaging his home to subsidize Marilyn's stay in New York.

Marilyn by Milton Greene, 1954. Greene had met Marilyn while on assignment for Look *magazine. His photographs combine Marilyn's glamour and sex appeal with a look of stylish sophistication that was new for her.*

Marilyn's genius as a photographer's model was seldom more apparent than in this Milton Greene session of 1956. Touching in their expressiveness . . .

. . . the photos reveal new facets of Marilyn's personality.
Like André de Dienes, Milton Greene came close to uncovering the
"real" Marilyn.

*Marilyn knew that her fame had been built on
Hollywood-style sex appeal, so she never entirely
abandoned that image.*

On April 8, 1955, Marilyn appeared on *Person to Person*, a popular television interview program hosted by noted broadcast journalist Edward R. Murrow. Murrow enjoyed a sterling reputation as a newsman, and being selected for *Person to Person* was both an honor and an ordeal for Marilyn. Murrow asked his questions from the CBS studios, but the program originated live from the guests' homes. Marilyn's interview was conducted out of the Greenes' home, with both Milton and Amy appearing on camera with the glamorous star. Marilyn was petrified by the thought of appearing on live television, but Amy Greene discreetly guided her through the interview. Among other things, Murrow inquired about Marilyn's move to the East Coast, her new production company, and her desire to act in dramatic roles. The program treated her defection from Twentieth Century-Fox as a positive decision, rather than as the impulsive act of a spoiled star.

By the summer of 1955, Marilyn was living in her New York apartment in the Waldorf-Astoria Towers. New York City represented a new life for her. She acquired new friends who respected her, new business associates who understood her desires to showcase her dramatic skills, and a new romance—with playwright Arthur Miller.

Marilyn had first met America's premier playwright in 1950, while on the set of *As Young as You Feel*. Though distraught at the time over the death of Johnny Hyde, Marilyn was honored to meet both Miller and director Elia Kazan. Actor Cameron Mitchell, who had costarred in the stage and film versions of Miller's *Death of a Salesman*, introduced Marilyn to the famous dramatist and the prominent director. A few days later, Marilyn ran into Miller at a Hollywood party, where the two struck up a friendship. Even at this time, Marilyn was quite taken with Miller. She supposedly gushed to Natasha Lytess, "It was like running into a tree! You know—like a cool drink when you've got a fever. You see my toe—this toe? Well he sat and held my toe and we just looked into each other's eyes almost all evening." The beautiful starlet and the wiry playwright exchanged letters and phone calls for some months, but Miller's marriage to college sweetheart Mary Slattery prevented any serious involvement.

When Miller heard that Marilyn had moved to New York City, he obtained her phone number from a mutual friend, and the two began secretly dating in 1955. Despite the fact that he was still living at home with his family, it was obvious that Miller's marriage was in trouble—if not over—by this time. If questioned about their relationship by a nosy reporter, the two quipped that they were just friends, but those who knew Marilyn claimed that she had had her sights set on Miller for some time.

Amy Greene (center) helped Marilyn through the Person to Person *interview in April 1955. Though Marilyn was stiff and subdued, the broadcast was the highest-rated* Person to Person *ever.*

Writer Truman Capote squired Marilyn around the dance floor of New York's El Morocco in the spring of 1955.

Though she did not set foot on a movie set from the fall of 1954 to the early months of 1956, Marilyn was quite busy in New York. She frequented bookstores and boutiques, visited her Hungarian analyst several times a week, and attended acting classes at the famed Actors Studio. Often, she was followed around the city by a group of ardent young fans who called themselves the Monroe Six. Consisting of a half-dozen teenagers just out of high school, the Six always seemed to be lingering near the foyer of her apartment building. They often figured out her schedule for the day, an accomplishment that both amazed and amused Marilyn. Eventually, each of the Monroe Six met their idol as well as many of Marilyn's friends and companions. Together with another fan, a lone wolf named Jimmy Haspiel, the Six put together a mass of off-the-record data on Marilyn's New York period—clippings, personal photographs, home movies, eyewitness remembrances—that would prove invaluable to later biographers. These dedicated fans respected Marilyn's privacy, never interfering with her errands or daily routine, and Marilyn was touched by their adoration. After she married Arthur Miller, she threw a party for them at Miller's Connecticut farm.

Much of Marilyn's time during this period was taken up with her burning ambition to become a serious actress, a goal shared by her new mentor Lee Strasberg. She had been introduced to Strasberg in early 1955 by Cheryl Crawford, a producer/director who was one of the founding members of the Actors Studio. Marilyn had confided in Crawford her intention of developing her dramatic skills, and Crawford had insisted she meet Strasberg.

Marilyn was an usherette at the March 9, 1955, benefit premiere of East of Eden. *The proceeds went to the Actors Studio. Here, Marilyn arrives at New York's Astor Theater.*

In the midst of a crowded New York party, Marilyn finds time for her own thoughts.

Lee Strasberg had been the artistic director of the Actors Studio since 1948 and had gained worldwide acclaim for the Method, a highly disciplined approach to acting based on the teachings of Konstantin Stanislavski. Strasberg had also belonged to the legendary Group Theatre, which served as an actors' training ground as well as a stage company known for its leftist politics and socially meaningful productions.

Though the Actors Studio grew out of the Group Theatre, it was not really an extension of it. The Studio only vaguely recalled the leftist political orientation that the Group had embraced wholeheartedly. Several former members of the Group Theatre would be called before the House Un-American Activities Committee (HUAC) in the early 1950s and accused of having Communist ties. The political background of the Group Theatre and the paranoia of HUAC would eventually affect Marilyn in a direct way. Arthur Miller, who had known several members of the Group Theatre, would be subpoenaed to testify before HUAC, and a Fox executive would pressure Marilyn about her association with him.

To Marilyn, New York meant the Actors Studio. In these photos, she arrives at the Studio . . .

. . . intent upon improving her skills and proving herself as a dramatic actress.

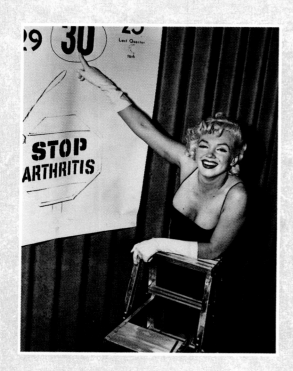

Marilyn gave her time to a 1955 charity benefit for Mike Todd's Arthritis and Rheumatism Foundation.

In March 1955, Marilyn was a first-nighter at Tennessee Williams's play, Cat on a Hot Tin Roof.

Because of her brief association with the Actors Lab in the late 1940s, Marilyn had already been exposed to some of the acting ideas advocated by Strasberg. Morris Carnovsky, who operated the Lab, had been a member of the Group Theatre and also used the teachings of Stanislavski as the basis for his own approach to acting. Despite those biographers and former associates who claim that Marilyn was lured by Strasberg and his wife Paula into the Actors Studio and brainwashed with the Method, Marilyn had leaned toward the Stanislavski approach as far back as her affiliation with both Carnovsky in the late 1940s and Michael Chekhov in the early 1950s.

Stanislavski had encouraged his pupils to examine their inner selves when attempting to understand their characters. According to the great Russian teacher, an actor should use his or her own past experiences and inner feelings to try to experience the emotions that the character will go through during the course of the play. The actor, in essence, emotionally lives out the experiences of the character. Lee Strasberg pushed the concept of the inner self a step further. He encouraged his students to not just act the role, but to *be* the character—to feel the same emotion the character feels and to live the experiences of the character. To arrive at that level of performance, Strasberg advocated the actor's total involvement with his or her self, as well as the actor's complete understanding of his or her motivations and inner feelings. Considering Marilyn's lifelong desire to uncover her identity, her disdain for those who confused her image with her true self, and her search for some inner peace regarding her worth as an individual, her attraction and ultimate devotion to Strasberg's teachings are understandable.

Strasberg regarded Marilyn's heightened sensitivity as a remarkable trait, especially considering her tragic childhood and her struggles in Hollywood. He believed her sensitivity and her luminous quality indicated a talent or gift that could be brought out through training. He worked with her privately for three months at his apartment, tutoring her on the ability to grasp what was happening inside the character she was playing and then recreate that emotion inside herself. He also improved her powers of concentration. After that time, she was allowed to join the regular classes at the Actors Studio, though she never became an official member.

During her tenure at the Actors Studio, Marilyn focused on her craft with such intensity that she won the respect and admiration of many of her fellow students. In addition to her class, which met twice a week, she sat in on other sessions at the Studio just to observe. Though she was terrified by performing in front of her class, she managed to work up a scene from *Anna Christie* for an audience of Studio members. Many were astonished at her skill and amazed at her depth.

Lee Strasberg has been quoted as saying that the two greatest acting talents he worked with were Marlon Brando and Marilyn Monroe. The statement is a testament to his faith in Marilyn, particularly in light of the heavyweight talents who studied with him—James Dean, Eli Wallach, Paul Newman, Montgomery Clift, Maureen Stapleton, Robert De Niro, Steve McQueen, Jane Fonda, and Al Pacino. Those biographers and former associates who accuse Strasberg of using the Method to cast a spell on his famous pupil have no understanding of Marilyn's longtime inclination in that direction, and they underestimate her dedication to her career.

Aside from training her in the Method, Lee and Paula Strasberg gave Marilyn some much-needed confidence that helped her to believe in herself. The couple had faith in Marilyn's abilities and encouraged her goals. "For the first time," Marilyn stated, "I felt accepted not as a freak, but as myself."

Eventually, Marilyn dismissed her longtime acting coach Natasha Lytess in favor of Paula Strasberg. Friends and acquaintances have often commented on Marilyn's tendency to cast aside trusted friends and old companions when she felt the forward momentum of her life carrying her beyond them. Lytess was bitter about Marilyn's decision, particularly because her foremost pupil arranged for the bad news to be relayed to her by an East Coast law firm. Marilyn was not hardened enough to perform the task herself. In an interview, Lytess claimed that Marilyn wouldn't even ask Twentieth Century-Fox to retain her services as a coach for other actors, though Fox may have wanted to get rid of her for their own reasons. Lytess died in 1964, just two years after Marilyn.

Marlon Brando, rumored to have had an affair with Marilyn, accompanied her to the December 1955 premiere of The Rose Tattoo.

On the town in 1956, with (from left), Sammy Davis, Jr., Milton Greene, and Mel Torme.

While Marilyn was living in New York, she was encouraged by the Strasbergs to enter analysis. Lee Strasberg believed analysis gave an actor an improved comprehension of his or her motivations and emotions. But Strasberg did not realize that Marilyn was involved in an inner struggle that analysis and the Method would never solve. Though experiencing one of the peak periods of her life and career, Marilyn was plagued by insomnia to such a degree that a bottle of Seconal was always in reach. More significantly, she was apparently unable to reconcile her image as sex goddess "Marilyn Monroe" with her own identity; she regarded "Marilyn Monroe" and her true self as two different entities. Actor Eli Wallach has remarked how she could walk through the streets of New York City and not be noticed and then, in a moment's time, make some inner adjustment to transform herself into the beautiful, breathy, and sensual movie star that everyone recognized. Heads turned, traffic stopped, and fans came running. "I just felt like being Marilyn for a moment," she would say.

Gradually, the strain of being the creation called "Marilyn Monroe" grew wearisome. Hindsight allows us to see Marilyn's ambivalent emotions in images such as this one. She began analysis in New York, and continued with it until the end of her life.

While Marilyn focused on improving her craft in New York, executives at Twentieth Century-Fox were battling with her lawyers and Milton Greene over her contract. After the extremely successful debut of *The Seven Year Itch* in June 1955, Fox pulled out all the stops in its efforts to re-sign Marilyn. With the critical and popular acclaim of the film, the studio realized that its biggest asset was Marilyn Monroe, the star who had generated the most box-office revenue for Fox in the past two years. In September, *Variety* reported that Fox was finally willing to meet Marilyn's unprecedented demands, which included story and director approval. Further, because Marilyn realized the importance of her physical appearance to the roles she played, she demanded and won cinematographer approval. In addition, her salary was boosted to $100,000 per film, and she was allowed to make films with independent producers and with other studios. Marilyn signed her fourth and final contract with Twentieth Century-Fox on December 31, 1955.

Though Marilyn's contractual difficulties with Fox during the mid-1950s have been widely documented, few accounts have adequately explained the magnitude of her victory and its ramifications to the film industry. Her new contract allowed her a measure of creative control that was considered revolutionary for an actor at that time. Her contract stipulated that she would appear in only top-notch productions, or "A-films." Her right to director and cinematographer approval set a precedent for other stars to follow.

Marilyn understood the value of working with directors who had not only talent but personal vision. She also understood the difference between a film that was genuinely suited to her, and one that merely exploited her good looks or marquee value. It was the difference between *Niagara*, in which her character's sexuality was the motivation for the action of the film, and *There's No Business Like Show Business*, in which she was cast merely to add some spice to a hack musical. Marilyn rightly realized that a succession of superficial films by assembly-line directors, in which she would play one sexy blonde after another, might cheapen her value as a star.

Some may find Fox's change of heart toward Marilyn hypocritical considering the bad publicity the studio had generated about her just a few months before. Did the executives at Fox not realize the extent of her popularity until *The Seven Year Itch*, or did they arrogantly assume she would return to the fold at some point? Actually, the situation was more complex than it might seem on the surface, and involves much more than Marilyn's dispute with Fox.

Victory was sweet in late 1955, when Twentieth Century-Fox acceded to Marilyn's demands and offered her a contract giving her unprecedented power and creative freedom.

At last, Marilyn had freed herself from the tyranny of the studio system.
Others stars, inspired by her tough negotiating style, soon followed her lead.
The powerless starlet had become a capable and self-assured businesswoman.

Hollywood underwent a number of significant changes during the 1950s, changes that would permanently alter the film industry. The studio system—designed to crank out formulaic films quickly and cheaply, and to give film studios almost absolute power over contract players and other creative people—began to decline during that era. Reasons for this decline include growing audience sophistication, the increasing popularity of television, and stars' unwillingness to sign contracts that limited their artistic and financial options. As the studio system withered, so did the enormous power that executives wielded over actors and directors. Prominent directors and established actors, fed up with the studios' profit-motivated decisions regarding their careers, began setting up their own production companies to make films with artistic merit, and to give themselves more equitable profit shares. Films using stage-trained directors and actors began to garner significant critical attention and box-office success.

Marilyn's relationship with the press improved. She handled a February 1956 Hollywood press conference with great skill. Gone were the snide remarks about her figure and about her ambitions. Marilyn had proved herself, and the press knew it.

The major studios clung desperately to outdated production methods in an effort to retain their dominance over the industry. It was those outdated methods—a dependence on quickly produced, low-budget B-films; a shortsighted tendency to assign big-name stars to minor films to boost the box-office potential—that Marilyn was fighting against. It was those outdated methods that could trap her in a succession of thankless roles in mediocre films. As the film companies began to lose money because of the changes in the studio system and because of the competition from television, they grasped at solutions they would not have considered just a few years earlier. After the financial success of *The Seven Year Itch*, Fox needed the bankability of Marilyn Monroe, and was willing to deal to get it.

Marilyn's victory not only became a landmark case but also established Marilyn Monroe as a force to be reckoned with. Suddenly, the press began to take Marilyn Monroe Productions seriously. In January of 1956, a year after some reporters had laughingly dubbed her "Bernhardt in a bikini," the *Los Angeles Mirror News* printed the following statement: "Marilyn Monroe, victorious in her year-long sitdown strike against 20th [sic] Century-Fox, will return to the studio next month with a reported $8,000,000.00 deal. Veterans of the movie scene said it was one of the greatest single triumphs ever won by an actress."

Marilyn, in high spirits from her victory over Fox, returned to Hollywood in February 1956 to star in the film adaptation of William Inge's acclaimed play *Bus Stop*, a property Milton Greene had purchased exclusively for her. Accompanied by coach Paula Strasberg and friend Amy Greene, Marilyn appeared more confident and serious than she had been when she last worked in Hollywood. At a press conference to announce her career plans, Marilyn fielded questions with wit and grace. Perhaps recalling how the media had distorted her comments about *The Brothers Karamazov*, Marilyn requested clarification on many questions and parried reporters' attempts to catch her off-guard. When one reporter hinted that her attire—a dark suit with a high collar—differed from her usual low-cut gowns and was perhaps meant to suggest a "new Marilyn," the actress neatly squashed the attempt to belittle her with the simple reply, "Well, I'm the same person. It's just a new suit."

For the first Marilyn Monroe Production, Milton Greene selected William Inge's popular play, Bus Stop. *Marilyn's costar was Don Murray.*

The cowboy woos his angel.

As the wan saloon singer Cherie, Marilyn gave a performance that was heartbreakingly good. With her here are Murray and Arthur O'Connell.

Marilyn's performance in *Bus Stop*, her first since her training with Strasberg, remains the finest of her career. In this classic film adaptation, Marilyn plays a sweet, talentless saloon singer who calls herself Cherie. Cherie hails from the Ozarks but is working her way across the Southwest toward Hollywood, where she hopes to be discovered and "get treated with a little respect, too." At a rowdy cowboy bar in Arizona, she meets a naive young rancher named Bo, played by Broadway actor Don Murray in his film debut. Bo has traveled to Phoenix not only to participate in the big rodeo but also to find "an angel" —that is, a wife to accompany him back to Montana. Despite Cherie's checkered past, Bo sees her as his angel, because she seems so fragile—"so pale and white." He is determined to marry her, though she rejects his bullying tactics. Only after his male pride is humbled, and he apologizes for his domineering manner, does Cherie respond to him. Only after he shows respect for her feelings does she accept his proposal.

Marilyn immersed herself in the role eagerly. She was adamant about the details that would contribute to the realism of the character, and promised to walk off the set if her demands weren't met. Her portrayal is vivid and affecting. As a singer, Cherie is hopeless, completely unaware of her lack of talent and ignorant of the pitfalls that are sure to befall her if she pursues her ill-considered course to "stardom." A luckless girl who wants desperately to better herself, Cherie aspires to more than she will ever attain.

The angel isn't sure she's ready to be a cowboy's bride.

Though highly sexual, the character has little of the glamour that characterized Marilyn's other parts. Marilyn chose to portray Cherie as a ragged, cheaply costumed waif. She rejected the original costume designs and insisted on wearing tattered odds and ends she found in the costume department. Milton Greene designed the pale, unflattering facial and body makeup that makes Cherie look tired and vaguely unhealthy. The singer's "hillbilly" accent, a key element of Marilyn's performance, was authentic and consistent. Her training with the Strasbergs had paid off. Marilyn didn't just act the role of Cherie—on-screen, she *became* Cherie.

Milton Greene created Cherie's ghostly pallor.

Cherie is caught by surprise in a scene that was eliminated from the final cut of Bus Stop.

Cherie longs most of all for respect.
Marilyn, too, struggled to gain respect.
Anyone who wishes an insight into Marilyn Monroe should watch Bus Stop;
in this film Marilyn came remarkably close to on-screen autobiography.

Upon hearing that Hollywood's most notorious blonde would star in *Bus Stop*, director Joshua Logan's initial reaction was, "Oh, no—Marilyn Monroe can't bring off *Bus Stop*. She can't act." In a later interview, Logan ate his own words, lamenting, "I could gargle with salt and vinegar even now as I say that, because I found her to be one of the greatest talents of all time." The mutual respect that existed between director and star was partially inspired by Logan's background. More active as a stage director than as a filmmaker, Logan was an acclaimed talent who had actually studied with Stanislavski at the Moscow Art Theater. (He also knew the Strasbergs well enough to ask Paula not to interfere with his direction on the set.) Like Marilyn, Logan was plagued by insomnia and exhaustion, so it is likely that he understood and was sympathetic to his star's personal problems.

The road to true love is a rocky one. From left, Robert Bray, Murray, Marilyn, O'Connell, Betty Field, and Hope Lange.

"Monroe is pure cinema."
—director Joshua Logan.

This publicity photo does not show the pathetic tears and runs in Cherie's costume— details that Marilyn herself insisted upon.

Though Marilyn's tardiness was not as evident during the production of this film, her new assertiveness often rubbed her costars the wrong way. For instance, she did not get along well with her leading man, Don Murray. The relationship came to a boil during the shooting of a specific scene, when Cherie becomes angered at Bo and hits him with the train of her costume, which the clumsy cowboy has inadvertently pulled off. In executing the action, Marilyn slapped Murray across the face with her sequin-studded costume with such force that blood was drawn. For reasons known only to herself and Murray, Marilyn refused to apologize.

Despite their differences during production, Murray has never harshly criticized Marilyn. "Marilyn Monroe had a childlike quality, and this was good and also bad," he recalled in a later interview. "Director Joshua Logan wanted a two-head close-up for *Bus Stop*, one of the first in CinemaScope. She broke me up when, in one of the frames, the top of my head was missing. 'The audience won't miss the top of your head, Don,' she said. 'They know it's there because it's already been established.' But, like children, she thought the world revolved around her and her thoughts. She was oblivious to the needs of people near her, and her thoughtlessness, such as being late frequently, [was] the bad side of it."

Momentarily lost in thought, Marilyn waits between set-ups on the Bus Stop *location.*

Marilyn's performance in *Bus Stop* garnered some of the best reviews of her career. The well-respected Bosley Crowther of *The New York Times* opened his commentary on the film with: "Hold onto your chairs, everybody, and get set for a rattling surprise. Marilyn Monroe has finally proved herself an actress in *Bus Stop*. She and the picture are swell." Arthur Knight, noted film historian and critic, raved, ". . . in *Bus Stop*, Marilyn Monroe effectively dispels once and for all the notion that she is merely a glamour personality, a shapely body with tremulous lips and come-hither blue eyes."

No fun at the rodeo.

Cherie's hopelessly amateurish yet highly erotic rendition of "That Old Black Magic" is a highlight of Bus Stop.

Though the critics may have been ready to accept the rebellious star's lofty ambitions and absence from the screen, Hollywood was not. In turmoil and desperately trying to maintain control over its actors, the film industry exacted its revenge for Marilyn's defection by failing to nominate her for an Academy Award. Critics had speculated in the trade papers that she would be nominated, and Logan, for one, felt she had been snubbed. He stated at the time, "[Marilyn's] performance that year was better than any other. It was a classical film performance." (The Best Actress Oscar for 1956 went to another Hollywood rebel, Ingrid Bergman, for her comeback role in *Anastasia*.)

In the end, the rough cowboy learns the importance of tenderness,
and Cherie gets some of the respect she's been dying for.
Though Marilyn and Don Murray did not get along particularly well,
their on-screen romance is a marvel of sweet naiveté.

Marilyn enjoyed a session with famed photographer Cecil Beaton in 1956.

The favorable tone of this Time *cover story was in marked contrast to the condescension the magazine had shown to Marilyn in the past.*

After the completion of *Bus Stop*, Marilyn returned to New York amid much speculation that she and Arthur Miller would soon marry. Miller had obtained a divorce from Mary Slattery in Reno, Nevada, while Marilyn had been officially divorced from DiMaggio since November 1955. Marilyn would soon be flying to London to begin work on her next film, and Miller had applied to regain his passport to accompany her. Holding up Miller's passport and complicating the marriage plans was a subpoena to appear before the House Un-American Activities Committee. Miller was subpoenaed by HUAC in June 1956, but his passport had been invalidated in 1954 because of suspected Communist leanings. His request for a new passport brought his name before HUAC once again; Congressman Francis Walter wanted Miller to testify about the alleged misuse of passports by American citizens.

Angered at this petty invasion of privacy, Miller accused Walter and the Committee of trying to capitalize on his relationship with Marilyn Monroe in order to increase publicity about HUAC's mission. Though a formidable group in the early 1950s, HUAC had lost much of its bite after the Red-baiting Wisconsin senator Joseph McCarthy finally overstepped the bounds of propriety in 1954, and was censured by a Special Senate Committee. The media had become less attentive without the headline-hungry senator around to stir things up, but Francis Walter was determined to press forward. He responded to Miller's accusations by trying to force the left-leaning playwright to identify the persons with whom he had attended a Communist meeting in 1947. During the proceedings Marilyn supported Miller both privately and publicly, telling newsreel reporters that she believed her future husband would win his case.

Miller was willing to sign a statement declaring that he was not and never had been a Communist, but he refused to inform on his friends or fellow writers. HUAC cited him for contempt of Congress, but Miller's contempt trial would not take place until the following year. Meanwhile, a wave of worldwide support for the acclaimed playwright from prominent artists and statesmen indicated to the State Department that HUAC's decision could hurt American credibility abroad. The State Department ordered the passport division to issue Miller a passport—quickly.

Years later, Marilyn would reveal that a certain executive from Twentieth Century-Fox—probably president Spyros Skouras—had pressured her to persuade Miller to cooperate with the Committee. When she told the executive that she stood firm behind Miller and his beliefs, he warned her that she could be through in the film industry. The executive's threats proved idle, however, because Marilyn's popularity eclipsed whatever slight damage that may been done by her indirect link to HUAC's investigation of domestic communism.

Between Miller's problems with Congress and the possibility of marriage between the Beauty and the Brain, the media attention hurled at Miller and Marilyn in the summer of 1956 became unbearable. Photographers camped out at Marilyn's apartment building in New York, ambushing her as she entered and exited. "Leave me alone, fellas," she would implore, as photos of her in old clothes and without makeup would be wired to papers across the country. Once a reporter attempted to rationalize his conduct to Miller by declaring, "We only bother you about this because people want to know." Miller's answer seemed to encapsulate his relationship with the press for the next few years: "It is your job versus my privacy. That's a remorseless conflict."

It was a conflict that Marilyn would come to know only too well in the years ahead.

Everybody was curious about "the new Marilyn Monroe"; The Saturday Evening Post ran a three-part series about Marilyn in May 1956. Writer Pete Martin later turned his articles into a book, Will Acting Spoil Marilyn Monroe?

Read Pete Martin's candid report on
"THE NEW MARILYN MONROE"

THE SATURDAY EVENING POST

THE EGGHEAD AND THE HOURGLASS

"If I were nothing but a dumb blonde, he wouldn't have married me."

MARILYN MONROE, ON ARTHUR MILLER

*Marilyn's marriage to playwright Arthur Miller seemed to be a fairy-tale
conclusion to the beautiful star's quest for happiness.
Marilyn was successful as an artist and married to a man she loved and respected.
For a time, the road ahead seemed smooth and clear.*

The double excitement of a possible Arthur Miller-Marilyn Monroe marriage and Miller's squabble with the House Un-American Activities Committee was sufficient to turn "the Egghead and the Hourglass" into the biggest news story of the summer of 1956. Articles that focused on the couple's romance seldom failed to mention Miller's HUAC headache, and stories that described Miller's fight with HUAC inevitably mentioned his relationship with Marilyn. Not only did the double-edged story make life difficult for Marilyn and her new fiancé in terms of increased press coverage, but it was only a matter of time before one of them inadvertently blurted out too much information about their plans. On June 21, 1956, during part of his testimony to HUAC, Miller revealed that he needed a passport to travel to England to discuss a possible London production of his play *A View from the Bridge*. He added, "And, I will be there with the woman who will then be my wife." Afterward, reporters in Washington nailed him on the latter half of his comment, insisting that Miller announce the date. The beleaguered writer could only mutter that the marriage would take place "very shortly."

When Marilyn and Miller faced the press in New York on June 22, 1956, Marilyn hugged her fiancé with such vigor that Miller happily warned, "I'll fall over." The reporters demanded to know the couple's wedding date.

What occurred next amounted to a virtual feeding frenzy among reporters and photographers as they relentlessly tracked Marilyn and Miller. When the press camped out in front of Marilyn's apartment building, the couple retreated to Miller's farm in Roxbury, Connecticut. Undaunted, the newsmen quickly set up shop on the doorstep of the Roxbury home. Miller persuaded them to leave only after he promised a news conference for the end of that week.

To escape scrutiny, the couple retreated to Miller's summer home in Connecticut. There, life assumed a more sedate air.

On June 29, the day of the scheduled press conference, hundreds of newsmen descended on the Miller property, trampling down the grass, even hanging from branches in the trees. In the early afternoon, the monotony of waiting for the famous couple was interrupted by the sound of a horrible crash. A few seconds later, a car carrying Marilyn and Miller sped up the driveway to the door. All of the car's occupants dashed quickly into the farmhouse. Miller's cousin, Morton, emerged from the house to announce that a terrible tragedy had occurred. A press car carrying reporter Mara Scherbatoff had crashed into a tree while in pursuit of Miller's car. Scherbatoff's teenaged driver, unfamiliar with the winding country roads, had been going too fast in an effort to keep pace with the Miller party. Scherbatoff, the New York bureau chief for *Paris-Match* magazine, was rushed to a nearby hospital. Her injury proved fatal, and she would die a short time later.

The peace would be short-lived, for the press descended en masse upon the farm just days after this photo was taken. The encounter brought not just commotion, but tragedy.

When Marilyn and Miller finally appeared on the lawn, accompanied by Miller's parents, they seemed outwardly calm, though some accounts of the day claim that Miller was livid at the press and Marilyn was almost hysterical over the accident. Perhaps in fear that the news media's zealousness could result in another tragedy, neither revealed an exact wedding date as originally promised.

Later that evening, Marilyn and Miller slipped across the state line to White Plains, New York, where they were married in a civil ceremony. Whether the accident had anything to do with the promptness of their decision is open to debate. Certainly, both wanted to put an end to the circus atmosphere. Two days later, on July 1, 1956, they were married in a Jewish ceremony at the home of Miller's agent. Lee Strasberg gave the bride away, and husband and wife celebrated with a reception for 25 close friends and associates.

Despite the tragedy that had preceded the event, Marilyn and Miller were ecstatic at their union, which is clearly evident in their wedding photographs. Marilyn not only adored her new husband, but she admired him for his talent and accomplishments. The usually reserved Miller was openly enamored of his beautiful and sensitive bride. Marilyn embraced family life, becoming quite close to her in-laws, Isidore and Augusta Miller. She referred to them as "Mom" and "Dad" almost immediately. Marilyn would remain close to her father-in-law until her death, visiting him on occasion and asking him to escort her to important functions. She also took instruction in the Jewish faith, and it was her decision to marry in a Jewish ceremony. In an interview from that period, Arthur Miller commented, "Until recently, I took my family for granted. But Marilyn never had one, and she made me appreciate what that means. When you see how much a family matters to her and you understand the depth of that feeling, you'd have to be an ox not to respond."

The newlywed bride happily regards her husband following the July 1 religious ceremony at Lewisboro, New York.

Attractive and prosperous,
the happy couple leave for a picnic shortly after their marriage.

Less than two weeks after their marriage, the celebrated couple departed for London, where Marilyn began work on her new film, a version of Terence Rattigan's play, *The Sleeping Prince*. Scheduled to produce and direct the sophisticated comedy was England's most celebrated actor, Laurence Olivier, who was also slated to star in the title role opposite Marilyn. Included among the distinguished supporting cast was Dame Sybil Thorndike.

July 14, 1956: Marilyn and Miller arrive in London for the shoot of The Prince and the Showgirl. *Marilyn's apparent good humor quickly faded.*

The contracts involving *The Sleeping Prince* had been signed in February of 1956. At that time, Olivier had flown to New York to join Marilyn for a press conference to announce his plans. Almost 200 reporters showed up for the event. The atmosphere was highly charged, not only because of the presence of Marilyn and Olivier, but because the bustle of activity was confined to a too-small room. After the questions commenced, one of the thin shoulder straps on Marilyn's black velvet dress broke, causing a sensation and diverting attention away from Olivier and the proposed film. A cynical press, more hostile toward Marilyn during this period than usual, accused her of intentionally breaking the strap. Marilyn denied the charge, angrily retorting, "How would you feel if something of yours broke in front of a whole room full of strangers?" Years later, Olivier would also contend that Marilyn's strap broke by design, not by accident. Whatever the case, Olivier got a telling preview of what working with Marilyn would be like, particularly in terms of the chaos related to her publicity and the tension generated between her desire to be a serious actress and her image as a movie star.

The film version of *The Sleeping Prince*, later retitled *The Prince and the Showgirl*, was the first independent project undertaken by Marilyn Monroe Productions. Milton Greene had purchased the property especially for Marilyn, and the unlikely team of Monroe and Olivier caused some chuckles in the press. Greene accompanied the Millers to London, as did Paula Strasberg and secretary Hedda Rosten. Olivier eventually clashed with all members of the Monroe entourage, though he managed to remain affable with Greene.

Marilyn is flanked by partner Milton Greene (left) and studio boss Jack Warner. Prince *would be released by Warner Bros.*

Problems began on the set almost immediately. Olivier had heard of the difficulties in working with Marilyn and had sought the advice of her former directors, including Joshua Logan. Logan advised Olivier not to be commanding or domineering, and not to raise his voice in anger; to do so would cause Marilyn to lose her confidence and thus her ability to work. Logan also reassured Olivier that Marilyn's performance would be worth any effort.

Whether Olivier did not fully grasp the meaning of Logan's advice or whether his temperament could not handle the frustration of working with such an insecure actress, he quite quickly brought out the worst in Marilyn. He could not comprehend her tendency to become distracted while taking direction, which he mistook for rudeness or denseness. He became frustrated with his costar, often raising his voice in anger and occasionally insulting her. Marilyn responded by arriving on the set hours late, sometimes failing to show up at all. Her tardiness was not the result of any vindictiveness on her part but was due to her innate fear and insecurity, which was heightened by Olivier's authoritative demeanor. Marilyn's fear of performing in front of Olivier and the other seasoned English actors in the cast virtually paralyzed her, a condition she sought to alleviate through prescription drugs.

The Prince and the Showgirl *aroused particular interest in Europe, where audiences were as enamored of Laurence Olivier as of Marilyn.*

During production, the film was known as The Sleeping Prince, *the name of the Terence Rattigan play upon which it was based.*

Olivier—technical and highly disciplined in his approach to acting—got on badly with Marilyn from the start. Marilyn respected Olivier, but quickly became intimidated.

Other disagreements developed from the presence on the set of Paula Strasberg, for whom Olivier had little respect as a coach. Olivier's approach to acting was the direct opposite of the Strasbergs' Method. A classically trained stage actor who tended toward impressive but conservative interpretations of Shakespeare, Olivier maintained a lifelong skepticism for the psychological undertones of the Method. Thus, in addition to any personality conflicts Olivier may have had with Marilyn, there were fundamental differences between the two in terms of how they approached their craft.

Paula Strasberg returned to the States before production was completed. Conflicting accounts of the episodes leading up to her departure blame her abrupt disappearance on everyone from Olivier to Miller. Strasberg eventually returned, and Marilyn's analyst was flown in to help her cope with the mounting tension on the set.

Marilyn knew that she had built her career on her sex appeal, but she strove by this time to temper her familiar image with an added subtlety and sophistication.

Despite Marilyn's aspirations to be a serious actress, glamour remained a vital part of her appeal.

Less sympathetic accounts of the behind-the-scenes turmoil tend to place blame on the Monroe camp. But to do so oversimplifies the situation. Olivier had directed only a handful of films prior to *The Prince and the Showgirl*, all of them adaptations of plays by Shakespeare. He was accustomed to directing classically trained actors and actresses much like himself. *The Prince and the Showgirl* was his first and last attempt at directing a vehicle for a bona fide American movie star. If Marilyn was ill-equipped to handle Olivier's rigid, stage-influenced directorial style, then Olivier was equally as inexperienced in interpreting popular material and handling screen idols.

The challenge of maintaining some semblance of a working relationship between Marilyn and Olivier fell on the shoulders of Milton Greene, while Arthur Miller assumed the duties of caretaker and manager for his unstable wife. Miller was often placed in the awkward position of having to explain or defend Marilyn's behavior. Often, after several hours of waiting on the set, Olivier would have an assistant phone Miller every few minutes at the couple's rented estate in Eggham to inquire as to when the cast and crew could expect to see Marilyn that day. Marilyn fell into a pattern of chronic insomnia, often becoming hysterical as the long nights wore on. Nightly vigils by her side became a common experience for Miller, who worked very little at his own craft during the four months of the film's production.

The romantic aspect of The Prince and the Showgirl *added a bleakly ironic note to the reality of Marilyn's insomnia and crippling insecurity. Further tension arose on the set because Olivier had little faith in Method acting or in Marilyn's devotion to it.*

Arthur Miller tried to mediate, but found himself squashed between two powerful wills. In late August, he escaped to the States for a ten-day visit with his children.

In the film, showgirl Elsie Marina transforms the authoritarian prince into an equitable ruler and more loving father. Alas, the real-life relationship between Marilyn and Olivier did not have as satisfying a resolution.

It was difficult for those living through the ordeal to have sympathy for Marilyn at the time, particularly after an episode in which she kept the elderly Dame Sybil Thorndike waiting on the set in full costume for hours. Thorndike, ever the gracious professional, refused to criticize the obviously ill Marilyn. Thorndike insisted, "We need her desperately. She's the only one of us who really knows how to act in front of the camera." After filming had been completed, Marilyn apologized to the entire cast and crew for her behavior.

Marilyn's unpleasant behavior and her increasing dependency on Miller to see her through each day strained their marriage considerably. The strain was magnified by Marilyn's discovery of Miller's personal notebook, an event that has been recounted so many times that its true impact on Marilyn is difficult to fully grasp. In the notebook, Miller had recorded some unflattering personal thoughts about Marilyn and his relationship with her. According to some accounts, his written comments revealed his disappointment in Marilyn's behavior during the production of *The Prince and the Showgirl*; in other accounts, he had compared Marilyn to his ex-wife. The story was embellished over time and through many retellings, even by Marilyn herself; one version claims that Miller's personal notes referred to his new bride as a "whore." Whatever the exact nature of Miller's jottings, some of Marilyn's closest friends, including the Strasbergs, maintained that her discovery was a heartbreaking one that signaled the beginning of the end of her marriage. Miller himself has always denied that this episode had any dire effect on the relationship.

Images such as this belie the strain that Marilyn felt during the film's production.

Marilyn's struggle did pay off, at least on screen; her conception of Elsie is fresh and beguiling.

The distinguished supporting cast of The Prince and the Showgirl *included Dame Sybil Thorndike (center).*

Despite Marilyn's personal and professional conflicts during production, *The Prince and the Showgirl* has become one of the actress's most acclaimed films. Well-crafted and beautifully photographed by Jack Cardiff, the movie tells the story of a turn-of-the-century American showgirl who has a brief encounter with the stuffy Grand Duke Charles, Prince Regent of Carpathia. During the course of their evening together, the unassuming chorine reunites the Prince with his estranged son, teaching the royal Romeo about mutual respect and fairness.

The improbable teaming of Marilyn Monroe and Laurence Olivier does nothing but enhance this sophisticated comedy. The innocence and sincerity of Marilyn's character, Elsie Marina, perfectly complements the pompousness of Olivier's Prince Regent. Marilyn's image, with its combination of innocence and sexuality, is once again used to splendid advantage. While Elsie's sexy exterior initially attracts the Prince to the Showgirl, her inner goodness and native wisdom transform him into a fair-minded father and more democratic leader.

Prince cinematographer Jack Cardiff did fine work on the picture; Marilyn seldom looked lovelier.

A break from the shoot was provided by the October 1956 London premiere of Miller's tragedy, A View from the Bridge.

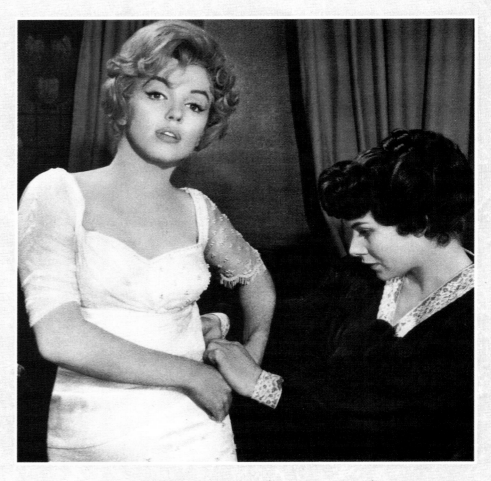

Marilyn's innate goodness and natural intelligence were two of her best qualities. In this regard, Marilyn and Elsie were quite similar.

Just as Cherie in *Bus Stop* bore similarities to the woman who portrayed her, so did Elsie Marina recall the real-life Marilyn—but in a far less tragic way. Whereas Cherie was searching for respect, just as Marilyn would for most of her career, Elsie's resemblance to the actress was tongue-in-cheek. Like Marilyn, Elsie is never on time, not even to meet her royal date; and, like Marilyn, Elsie is repeatedly described as childlike. Also, just as Marilyn's strap had broken at the press conference with Olivier, Elsie's dress strap breaks in the presence of the Prince. In real life, Marilyn's insecurities and bad habits caused delays and frustration; on the screen, these same qualities were presented as endearing. The fusion of Marilyn Monroe with the characters she played was something that Marilyn personally detested, but in *The Prince and the Showgirl* and *Bus Stop*, it may have helped her fans accept the less gracious aspects of her real-life personality—many of which were reported and exaggerated in the press.

Following the European release of The Prince and the Showgirl, *Marilyn proudly accepted Italy's David di Donatello Prize. Actress Anna Magnani watches.*

The film's depiction of backstage life is charming.

At London's Empire Theatre on October 29, 1956, Marilyn was presented to Queen Elizabeth. Standing at Marilyn's right is actor Victor Mature.

Marilyn's involvement in *The Prince and the Showgirl* earned her worldwide attention. Before the film was completed, she was asked to attend a Royal Command Film Performance before Queen Elizabeth. Along with several other film stars, Marilyn was presented to the Queen, who complimented the famous actress on her curtsy. After the film was released to much acclaim, particularly in Europe, Marilyn won Italy's David di Donatello Prize for Best Foreign Actress of 1958, as well as France's Crystal Star Award for Best Foreign Actress. Both awards are considered the equivalent of the Oscar, but Marilyn's chance for the real thing was denied her, as she was once again passed over by Hollywood at Academy Award-nomination time.

The ordeal of The Prince and the Showgirl *finally ended. On November 21, 1956, Marilyn and Miller said their goodbyes to Olivier and his wife, actress Vivien Leigh (far left). Contrary to her usual tardiness, Marilyn arrived at the airport 50 minutes early.*

Marilyn's first public appearance after returning home was at the December 1956 benefit premiere of Baby Doll. *Proceeds of the event went to the Actors Studio. Marilyn had lobbied for the film's title role, which went to newcomer Carroll Baker.*

Upon their return to the States, Marilyn and Miller retreated to the privacy of a rented cottage in Amagansett, Long Island. Miller completed a few short stories, including "Please Don't Kill Anything," inspired by Marilyn's inability to tolerate suffering in any living creature, and "The Misfits." Marilyn enjoyed some peaceful days and restful nights at Amagansett, though she still suffered frequent bouts of insomnia. After the stressful experiences in London, the newlyweds were determined to focus on their life together. Away from the pressures of her career and the fear that few in the film industry respected her, Marilyn was heard to say, "Movies are my business, but Arthur is my life."

A handful of disappointing episodes interrupted the couple's secluded existence. In May 1957, Miller's contempt of Congress trial ended. Marilyn told newsmen she was confident her husband would win his case, but Miller was convicted on two counts of contempt. He received a 30-day suspended sentence and a $500 fine. Though the penalty was hardly devastating, Miller had fought hard to be acquitted as a matter of principle. He chose to appeal the conviction, which was finally overturned in August 1958.

The spring of 1957 brought another milestone, as Marilyn severed her personal and business relations with partner Milton Greene. Their friendship had lost much of its initial closeness after her marriage to Miller, while their business association rapidly deteriorated during the production of *The Prince and the Showgirl*. During the group's stay in London, Greene had attempted to organize a British subsidiary of Marilyn Monroe Productions, an act that Miller interpreted as conducting business behind Marilyn's back. In addition, Marilyn resented Greene's congenial relationship with Olivier, and she suspected him of shipping antiques back to the States and billing the charges through Marilyn Monroe Productions. After returning to New York, communication between the two partners disintegrated completely. Marilyn had trusted Greene in such an idealistic manner that any deal he attempted for his personal benefit— though perfectly legitimate—was considered by her to be a betrayal. Marilyn, with the help of Miller and his lawyers, decided to break with Greene and sue him for control of Marilyn Monroe Productions. Greene eventually settled the matter by accepting a mere $100,000 for his share of the company. Whatever the reasons behind the dissolution of the Greene-Monroe partnership, the ambitious photographer cannot be faulted for the work he did on Marilyn's behalf. Both *Bus Stop* and *The Prince and the Showgirl*—properties Greene personally selected for Marilyn—were finished within their budgets, and both films were considered critical and popular successes.

The most devastating blow to Marilyn's emotional and mental state occurred during the summer of 1957. Marilyn had become pregnant in June, a stroke of good fortune that left her ecstatic. She adored children and had always been active in children's charities. She was devoted to Arthur Miller's two children by his former marriage and remained close to DiMaggio's son until her death. Miller once observed, "To understand Marilyn best, you have to see her around children. They love her; her whole approach to life has their kind of simplicity and directness." Sadly, she could not carry her own baby to full term. A few weeks into her pregnancy, she was in such physical agony that Miller called an ambulance to rush her to Doctor's Hospital in New York. Doctors discovered that her pregnancy was tubular, and were forced to surgically terminate it.

Beginning in early 1957 and continuing off and on into the summer of 1958, Marilyn and Miller rejuvenated themselves at Amagansett, Long Island. For the first time in months, Miller had the time and energy to write.

Marilyn lets the seashore work its healing magic.

In the weeks following her loss, Marilyn grew increasingly despondent. In an effort to bolster her spirits, Miller discussed his plans for turning "The Misfits" into a suitable dramatic script for her. He planned to focus on the female character Roslyn, who is mentioned only in the dialogue of the short story, and make her a central part of the action for the film. Marilyn was pleased by the idea but could not fully shake her depression. Her dependency on medication to sleep—and perhaps escape—increased significantly. At least once during this period she sought oblivion by swallowing too much medication, though whether she did so as a destructive act or as an attempt to sleep through her anguish can only be surmised. Marilyn's spirits remained depressed, and she would make no public appearances until the end of January 1958.

The June 13, 1957, premiere of The Prince and the Showgirl *was one of Marilyn's last public appearances until early the following year.*

Marilyn and Miller arrived at the Prince *premiere amid great hoopla and ceremony.*

Goalie, beware! Marilyn opens a soccer game at Brooklyn's Ebbets Field in 1957.

While in England, Miller had sold his beloved Connecticut residence. When a 300-acre farm near his previous Roxbury home went on the market, Miller wasted no time in purchasing it. The reserved, serious-minded writer loved the quiet life of the country, though Marilyn often longed for the stimulation of New York. The couple divided their time between the solitude of their country farm and Marilyn's new apartment in the city. Miller maintained studies at both residences, where he continued to work on his script adaptation of "The Misfits."

After *The Prince and the Showgirl* wrapped in the fall of 1956, Marilyn did not appear on a movie set until the summer of 1958. Almost two years had passed between projects, during which time Marilyn had attempted—not too successfully—to put some of her personal demons behind her. On August 4, 1958, Marilyn began work with director Billy Wilder on *Some Like It Hot*—a production fraught with horrendous fighting, debilitating health problems, heartbreaking disappointments, and harsh accusations. Yet, the film would also be her greatest financial success—her most popular triumph. The tragedy of her life was that such extreme highs and lows were so often wrapped in the same package.

A spoof of the gangster era in Chicago, *Some Like It Hot* tells the story of two musicians who accidentally witness a gangland shooting not unlike the St. Valentine's Day Massacre. To escape Chicago and possible retaliation by the mob, the two buddies, played by Tony Curtis and Jack Lemmon, don dresses and join an unsuspecting all-girl orchestra headed for Florida. Marilyn costars as the band's ukulele player, a kooky singer named Sugar Kane, who befriends the two new "girls." The skirt-chaser played by Curtis falls for Sugar, but the ambitious blonde has confided that her life's goal is to marry a millionaire. This farce of false identities takes a complex twist when Curtis embarks on a second masquerade as a wealthy oil magnate in order to woo the beautiful Sugar. A comical subplot highlights Jack Lemmon's talent for physical comedy: While disguised as a woman, Lemmon is aggressively courted by aging millionaire Osgood Fielding III, played by the rubber-faced comic actor Joe E. Brown. Through it all, the two male protagonists must keep watchful eyes open for the gangsters, who are determined to track them down and rub them out.

Marilyn realized early on that, as originally conceived, Sugar Kane was little more than a "straight man" for the antics of the two male characters. She requested that Wilder and his writing collaborator I.A.L. Diamond add bits and pieces to the script that would develop Sugar Kane's personality and allow the character to be a more active participant in the fun.

One of the scenes that Wilder and Diamond rewrote is the first appearance of Sugar, captured as she hurriedly wobbles on high heels to catch a train. The rewrite allowed Marilyn to engage in a bit of physical comedy, for as Sugar shimmies along the platform, a sudden blast of steam noisily bursts from the train and across her undulating bottom. The cheerfully vulgar situation and Sugar's surprised reaction provide the audience with a good laugh, and establish immediately the freewheeling nature of Marilyn's portrayal.

Rested after a layoff of nearly two years, Marilyn returned to moviemaking in the summer of 1958.

Marilyn's comeback vehicle was Some Like It Hot, *perhaps her greatest triumph. By any standard, it is a comic masterpiece.*

Marilyn was pleased with the new scene that Wilder and Diamond came up with. She wanted her character to hold her own in the broad physical comedy intrinsic to a plot involving two men masquerading as women. By vigorously playing Sugar as a bona fide kook instead of as just another two-dimensional dumb blonde, Marilyn simultaneously exploited and expanded her image.

Some Like It Hot was photographed in black and white, a decision that was a major point of contention with Marilyn at the outset. Though this film was an independent project distributed by United Artists, Marilyn's most recent Fox contract stipulated that all her movies be shot in color. She felt that she photographed best in color, and she balked at the plan to shoot her first film in two years in black and white. Marilyn relented when Wilder showed her color tests of Lemmon and Curtis in their heavy makeup, which assumed a ghastly green tint on film.

On location at California's Hotel del Coronado, Marilyn shares a happy moment with costar Joe E. Brown.

Billy Wilder, director and co-screenwriter of Some Like It Hot, *gives his star a bit of advice during the filming of the famous upper-berth sequence.*

Although photographed in black and white, the film sacrifices none of Marilyn's considerable allure.

The plot of Some Like It Hot—*in which a pair of male musicians disguise*
themselves as women in order to elude mobsters—is inspired farce.
Marilyn's singing is an added treat. Here, Marilyn is joined by
(from left) costars Tony Curtis and Jack Lemmon, and
supporting player Dave Barry.

Early in his career, Tony Curtis's appearances in
B-movies won him legions of young female fans. Later, he was convincing in prestige dramas.
In Some Like It Hot, Curtis proved himself a clever and enthusiastic comic actor.
For this famous sequence, he did a dead-on impression of Cary Grant.

As the production continued, Wilder realized that Marilyn's concerns for her character and the quality of the film were the least of his worries. Marilyn's tardiness and absences held up production and pushed the film over its budget, and had a near-disastrous effect on the morale of the cast and crew. Sometimes hours late, Marilyn kept costars Lemmon and Curtis waiting on the set in full costume and heavy makeup. When she was working, dozens of takes were sometimes required for her to conquer even the simplest of lines. The need for repeated takes had always been a problem with Marilyn when she felt nervous or insecure. Her drug use and increasing dependence on alcohol during this period greatly magnified the problem. Her inability to master such lines as "Where is that bourbon?" in less than 40 takes has become the stuff of movie legend. Her costars, particularly Curtis, were upset during these episodes, not only because her problems made for some very long days, but also because their performances became less effective as the number of takes increased. Curtis's anger at Marilyn over such delays caused him to ridicule or criticize her after filming was completed. His notorious quote about Marilyn—"Kissing her is like kissing Hitler"—indicates the degree of tension and resentment that permeated the set.

Though Marilyn's personal troubles had intensified by this time in her career, she easily carried off the scenes shot at the Hotel del Coronado.

Regrettably, these tales lead fans to assume that Marilyn was confused or flustered every day of the shoot, which is untrue. Certain sequences, including the exterior beach scenes shot at California's Hotel del Coronado, were mastered in only one or two takes.

Wilder confers with Marilyn and (barely visible) Paula Strasberg, whose influence with Marilyn was enormous.

Jack Lemmon, decked out as "Daphne," is more than a little surprised to see his friend masquerading as an oil millionaire.

Director Billy Wilder's relationship with Marilyn, which began with *The Seven Year Itch*, deteriorated during the production of *Some Like It Hot*. After the shoot was completed, Wilder released some disparaging remarks about her to the press. The hard-bitten director, who had suffered muscle spasms in his back during production, remarked to a reporter that since the film was finished, "[I can] look at my wife again without wanting to hit her because she was a woman." The comment struck Marilyn and Miller as being particularly cruel because Marilyn suffered another miscarriage after production was completed. Reportedly, the miscarriage resulted from the physical and emotional strain of making the film.

Marilyn and Tony Curtis rehearse the "Shell Oil" scene.

A cute but misleading publicity still; in the film, it is revealed (to great comic effect) that Curtis has been soaking in the tub fully clothed.

Much of the humor of Jack Lemmon's impersonation of a woman arises from his angular, un-curvy physique. True to the film's flapper-era setting, Marilyn's Sugar Kane compliments "Daphne" for her enviably flat chest.

Two years later, at a party celebrating Wilder's next film, *The Apartment*, Marilyn and the great director mended their differences. Unsubstantiated comments and rumors circulated at the time, claiming that Wilder was willing to work with Marilyn on a third project. That Wilder thought Marilyn brought something special to the screen is confirmed by his comments praising her "high voltage" and her "luminous" presence. Of Marilyn's performance in *Some Like It Hot*, the director remarked, "Marilyn Monroe was very sensitive, difficult, and disorganized. . . . In some cases you had to match shots from different takes to make it seem as though she were giving a performance; but there were stretches when she was absolutely phenomenal; one of the great comediennes."

Marilyn and Curtis wait
between set-ups. Paula
Strasberg stands by.

Marilyn chats with a
member of the crew.

Curtis prepares to launch
himself into a bit of
physical comedy.

Regrettably, Marilyn and
Jack Lemmon never again
costarred.

Since Marilyn's death, Wilder's opinion of the legendary actress has remained ambivalent, often contradictory. His conflicting comments reveal not only his admiration for Marilyn's talents but also a deep-seated anger over her unprofessional habits and disregard for her costars. Wilder's most telling comment about Marilyn was recorded in columnist Earl Wilson's 1971 book, *The Show Business Nobody Knows*. The director reminisced, "I miss her. It was like going to the dentist, making a picture with her. It was hell at the time, but after it was over, it was wonderful."

In retrospect, the comedic brilliance of *Some Like It Hot* makes irrelevant the torture that was involved in its creation. Some film historians regard the picture as Wilder's masterpiece, while others name it as the finest American comedy of the sound era. As a spoof of the gangster-film genre, it is unparalleled. Monroe biographers generally regard the film as the peak of Marilyn's acting career; the innocent aspect of her image was never put to better use, and is a key element in the film's success.

The essential innocence of Sugar Kane provides a wonderful counterpoint to the more cynical nature of the character played by Tony Curtis.

Sugar's tête-à-tête in the upper berth with "Daphne" is a gem of double-entendre dialogue.

The sunny, windblown Marilyn has faint echoes of the outdoorsy cover-girl model of ten years earlier.

Some Like It Hot epitomizes the themes Wilder explored throughout his career. Many of his pictures revolve around some sort of con or swindle—a murder-for-profit scheme in *Double Indemnity*; a reporter's opportunistic manipulation of tragedy in *The Big Carnival*; the double lives of adulterous business executives in *The Apartment*. Though Wilder's characters are seldom thoroughly bad, they are often cynical, corrupted, or interested only in personal gain, often at the expense of the feelings or well-being of others. Wilder typically underlined their deceitful intentions by providing a sharply contrasting character, an innocent figure who is fascinated or victimized by the world's corruption.

Marilyn needed interminable takes to wrap up the sequence on board the millionaire's yacht. Tony Curtis's patience hung by a slender thread.

A witty ad campaign highlighted the picture's powerhouse cast.

In *Some Like It Hot*, Sugar's sincerity exposes the chicanery of the male characters. The two musicians attempt to deceive the women in the orchestra with their masquerade, while Curtis misleads Sugar further with his oil magnate's disguise. On a more farcical level, Lemmon's character deceives millionaire Osgood Fielding III by leading him on sexually. Although Sugar—momentarily swept up in the thrill of being romanced by an apparent oil millionaire—makes a halfhearted attempt to pass herself off as a society girl, she never fails to freely reveal her thoughts and feelings, even as the two male characters struggle to conceal theirs. Wilder's ironic, sometimes caustic view of life is revealed at the end of the story, when all of the deception is exposed, yet few consequences are suffered. Curtis's character still wins the affection of Sugar, while Osgood Fielding expresses little concern that Lemmon's character is actually a man. "Nobody's perfect," deadpans Joe E. Brown, giving voice to Wilder's acceptance of a less-than-ideal world.

Understandably, Curtis was not crazy about Marilyn. Still, Some Like It Hot *will certainly be his most enduring film.*

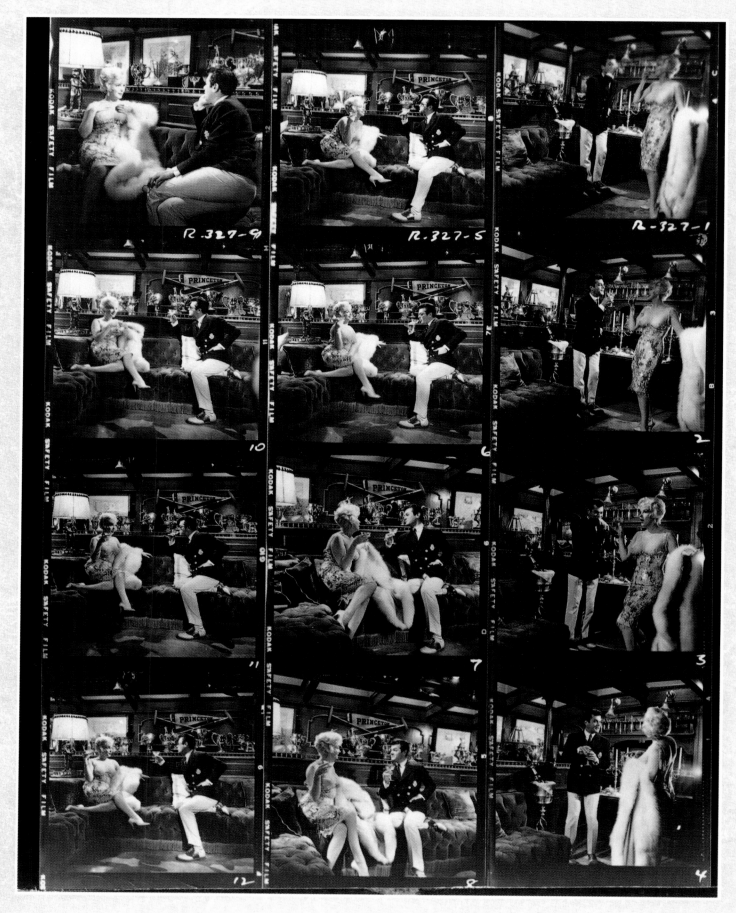

The yacht sequence of Some Like It Hot
is every bit as bubbly and animated as these images suggest.

Jack Lemmon's enthusiastic and brilliantly funny performance is a high point of *Some Like It Hot*, but it is Marilyn's luminous presence and witty interpretation of Sugar that make the film a special one. Though Sugar is vitally important to the picture, and the image of Marilyn Monroe essential to convey the innocence necessary for the role, Marilyn managed to enrich the character even further. Her insistence on making her characters real—a result of her Method training—added a human quality to Sugar.

Some Like It Hot depended on the actors' ability to nimbly handle physical humor and broad farce; despite their personal differences, Marilyn, Curtis, Lemmon, and the rest of the cast (which includes veterans George Raft and Pat O'Brien, cleverly spoofing their own images) faced the challenge. Together, they created an American film classic. As time passes and memories of the turbulence of the production fade, it will be the film itself that will be remembered. *Some Like It Hot*—and Marilyn's wonderful performance—will endure.

Some Like It Hot was nominated for six Academy Awards, though Marilyn was overlooked in the Best Actress category. The film won only one Oscar—for costume design in a black-and-white film. Still, Marilyn's performance did not go totally unrewarded; she won a Golden Globe Award as best actress in a comedy or musical and, once again, received sparkling reviews.

Because of Marilyn's insistence that her role be fleshed out, and because of her success with the Method, the star's portrayal of Sugar Kane is dimensional and sweetly affecting.

Some Like It Hot *can be viewed as a showcase for the brilliance of Jack Lemmon, but the film's special glow was provided by Marilyn.*

As the decade drew to a close, the contradiction between the turmoil of Marilyn's personal life and the fame of her stardom became more dramatic than ever before. Two ill-fated pregnancies and an increasing dependency on the escape offered by drugs and alcohol wore Marilyn down, making her distressed in private and even more timid with strangers. In June 1959, she elected to have surgery to increase her chances of having a child. The effort would prove futile, leaving her insecure about her womanhood.

In her public life, Marilyn's celebrity reached such proportions that she was invited to meet Soviet premier Nikita Khrushchev during his 1959 visit to America. Marilyn flew to Los Angeles to join other stars and studio luminaries at a special luncheon arranged by Twentieth Century-Fox. If the private Marilyn doubted her identity as a woman, the public Marilyn affirmed it for her. The movie star would remark after her luncheon with the powerful world leader, "Khrushchev looked at me like a man looks at a woman."

*Marilyn gamely waves to fans as she leaves New York's
Lenox Hill Hospital in June 1959 following elective
surgery intended to increase her chances of becoming
a mother. The effort would prove unsuccessful.*

*The troubled Hollywood goddess summoned her natural exuberance
for a 1959 session with photographer Philippe Halsman.
Halsman had photographed Marilyn twice before, in 1949 and in a 1952 session
that produced the actress's first Life cover.
By 1959, world famous but plagued by invisible demons, Marilyn
was a quite different person than the hopeful starlet Halsman had known.*

FINAL SCENES

"It might be kind of a relief to be finished. It's sort of like, I don't know what kind of yard dash you're running, but then you're at the finish line and you sort of sigh—you've made it! But you never have—you have to start all over again."

MARILYN MONROE

During the shoot of The Misfits, *the last film that she would complete,*
Marilyn struggled with her depression and failing marriage.
But in at least one moment in the Nevada desert,
she may have achieved a kind of peace.

Arthur Miller completed the screenplay for *The Misfits* in 1958, about the time Marilyn began working on *Some Like It Hot.* The Millers assumed that as soon as Marilyn wrapped production on the Wilder comedy, they could begin shooting *The Misfits.* Miller had already lined up a powerful ensemble to work on the film: John Huston agreed to direct; Clark Gable, Eli Wallach, and Montgomery Clift were set to costar; and publishing executive Frank Taylor—Miller's neighbor and friend—was enlisted as producer. Taylor, Miller, and Marilyn formed their own production company for the purposes of producing the film. All parties were eager to begin because Miller's dramatic and thoughtful script promised to showcase Marilyn's acting talents to their fullest extent.

Twentieth Century-Fox quickly burst everybody's bubble with the news that Marilyn needed to fulfill her contractual obligation to the studio. Marilyn had promised Fox four films in seven years, but she had completed only one to date, *Bus Stop.* Fox was pressuring her to do a film for the studio before embarking on another independent feature. Marilyn finally agreed to star in a frothy musical comedy entitled *Let's Make Love,* which apparently was the least objectionable of the scripts Fox had to offer.

In January 1960, Marilyn readied herself to begin work on Let's Make Love. *She relaxes here with Arthur Miller, actress Simone Signoret, and costar Yves Montand.*

Marilyn asked her husband to improve the script with an extensive rewrite, but even the Pulitzer Prize-winning author could add little to bolster the slight story. Miller despised the idea of rewriting a trivial film script, particularly one he described as "not worth the paper it was typed on." Still, he tried to tailor Marilyn's role to her talents and image. Gregory Peck, who was scheduled to costar, bowed out when he read Miller's rewrite, leaving the production without a leading man. Cary Grant, Charlton Heston, and Rock Hudson were asked to step in, but all turned down the Norman Krasna-Arthur Miller scenario. Finally, French actor Yves Montand agreed take the role.

Montand and his wife, actress Simone Signoret, greatly admired Arthur Miller and shared certain political beliefs with him. The couple had even appeared in the French film version of Miller's *The Crucible,* which had been adapted by Jean-Paul Sartre. Marilyn had seen Montand in his one-man show on Broadway and was taken by his Gallic charm. The Millers were eager to befriend the Montands, and the four were often seen together when *Let's Make Love* first went into production in mid-February of 1960.

Miller noticed that Marilyn's moods began to shift quite rapidly during this period. Though she seemed to accept the tragedy of her most recent miscarriage, she was not altogether happy with married life. Often, her disappointment took the form of vindictiveness or obvious disrespect toward her husband. She also began to alienate herself from many of her New York friends and acquaintances. On a more positive note, her drug intake decreased as she stopped sedating herself during the day—at least on some days. Still, according to some accounts, she was taking more drugs than her new California psychiatrist, Dr. Ralph Greenson, thought safe.

Let's Make Love *is a well-mounted trifle that was annoyingly coy even for its day. The drama that took place away from the set—Marilyn's affair with Montand—was infinitely more interesting than the film itself.*

Soon after shooting of *Let's Make Love* got underway, both Miller and Signoret were called away from Los Angeles, leaving Marilyn and Montand alone. Whether the two stars began their love affair at this time, or whether it had developed earlier, is unknown. Montand has always claimed that Marilyn was the aggressor; if so, he did little to discourage her. Though Miller returned to Hollywood briefly, he did not stay, preferring to weather out his marital problems back east. If reports in the gossip columns are any indication, the two stars did little to hide their affair. Marilyn's psychiatric care was part of Hollywood gossip at the time, so those columnists who were generally friendly with Marilyn took Montand to task for taking advantage of her.

On the set, Marilyn cooperated with director George Cukor and other cast members—agreeable behavior that was in stark contrast to her conduct on her last two productions. It is likely that Marilyn was emulating Montand's professionalism, a quality she admired in him. Montand took at least part of the credit for her improved attitude when he remarked, "She's got so she'll do whatever I ask her to do on the set. Everyone is amazed at her cooperation, and she's constantly looking to me for approval."

Much of the credit, however, must go to George Cukor, an "actor's director" who enjoyed a repuation for bringing out the best in his female stars; Katharine Hepburn was just one of the legendary figures who admired Cukor's sensitive treatment of female characters. He avoided a reliance on visual technique and concentrated instead on the blocking (movement), characterization, and dialogue delivery of his stars. In effect, the actor was Cukor's basic mode of expression. It is quite possible that Marilyn felt Cukor was more sympathetic to the character she was playing than other directors had been to her roles in the past. The veteran director was probably at least partially responsible for her cooperative attitude. Unfortunately, though Marilyn did not impede the shooting schedule, two Hollywood strikes—first by the Screen Actors Guild and then by the Screen Writers Guild—held up production of *Let's Make Love* for over a month.

After the film was completed, Montand broke off his affair with Marilyn. Apparently, he had no intention of leaving Simone Signoret. He stated publicly, "[Marilyn] has been so kind to me, but she is a simple girl without any guile. Perhaps I was too tender and thought that maybe she was as sophisticated as some of the other ladies I have known . . . . Had Marilyn been more sophisticated, none of this ever would have happened . . . . Perhaps she had a schoolgirl crush. If she did, I'm sorry. But, nothing will break up my marriage."

During the summer of 1960, when Marilyn was shooting *The Misfits* and Montand was back in Los Angeles, Marilyn tried to get in touch with her Frenchman but to no avail. Finally, following the completion of her film, Marilyn met Montand at Idlewild Airport in New York. In the back seat of her limousine, the two bid each other farewell.

The affair itself did not destroy Marilyn's marriage with Miller. It was merely another step toward its gradual disintegration. However, considering Marilyn's increasingly fragile state and growing tendency to disengage herself from everyday existence, the relationship with Montand was a destructive event in her life.

This scene from Let's Make Love *seems to encapsulate the personal unhappiness that Marilyn was feeling at the time.*

Despite the real-life sparks generated by the Monroe-Montand liaison, *Let's Make Love* is a distinctly unengaging musical comedy, and remains Marilyn's weakest starring vehicle. Montand played billionaire Jean-Marc Clement, a world-famous playboy whose eyebrows are raised when he learns of a theater troupe's plan to satirize him in a musical revue. Intending to stop production, Clement appears at a casting call for the play, where he is immediately smitten by the character played by Marilyn, a singer-dancer named Amanda Dell. Not realizing Clement's true identity, the director hires the billionaire to play himself in the show. Clement uses the opportunity to court Amanda, who continually expresses her distaste for irresponsible, playboy-type billionaires. Predictably, Amanda falls in love with Clement, whom she believes to be merely a starving actor. The film's cast included Tony Randall and Wilfrid Hyde-White in supporting roles, and spotlighted Milton Berle, Gene Kelly, and Bing Crosby in cameo appearances as themselves.

These ingredients, though contrived, are far from hopeless. Unfortunately, the slight script makes use of Marilyn's image but not her talent. Lacking believable characterization and subtlety of treatment, the film merely recycles famous Monroe bits from other movies, and borrows elements of her life that fans would readily recognize. Marilyn's character, Amanda, is a musical comedy actress, but she attends night school to better herself. Amanda is a proponent of Method acting, which is indicated when she instructs Clement to pretend he owns a limousine in order to get in the proper frame of mind to portray a rich man. One of Amanda's musical numbers puts her in a white, flouncy, V-necked dress, which is blown upward during the course of the number—an obvious reference to *The Seven Year Itch*. Together, these bits and pieces add up to very little.

The script of Let's Make Love *offered very little on which Marilyn could hang a characterization. This, coupled with her unusually subdued performance, is sufficient to turn the film into a Technicolor exercise in somnambulism.*

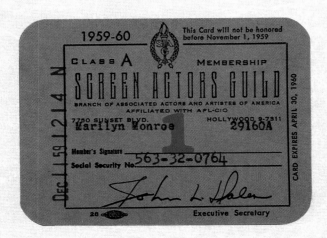

Marilyn's membership card in the Screen Actors Guild, valid during the shoot of Let's Make Love.

Despite the flimsiness of *Let's Make Love*, Marilyn's sexuality and spark are evident in one of the film's musical numbers—the scorching "My Heart Belongs to Daddy." Aside from that highlight, only Milton Berle's routine with Montand, in which the veteran comic tries to teach the Frenchman about American comedy, stands out. Though most Monroe biographers have deemed the film a critical and popular failure, first-run reviews of *Let's Make Love* are actually mixed. In addition, there is no indication that the film crashed at the box office, though it certainly was not the popular hit that Fox executives had counted on.

In July 1960, principal production finally began on *The Misfits*, which was Miller's valentine to Marilyn. Directed by John Huston, written by Arthur Miller, and starring Marilyn Monroe, Clark Gable, Montgomery Clift, and Eli Wallach, *The Misfits* promised to be a powerhouse film as well as Marilyn's chance to prove her acting abilities. In retrospect, both statements are true. A haunting film with beautiful imagery, *The Misfits* is not only a provocative parable about the vanishing West but a splendid showcase for Marilyn, cast in the most serious and challenging role of her career. At the time, however, the movie seemed doomed by Marilyn's personal struggles, which cast a pall over the production, and threatened to overshadow the power of the film itself.

The Misfits is a sophisticated allegory about three men, alienated from society and the last of a dying breed, who belong to a West long since gone. Nevada cowboys Gay Langland (Gable) and Perce Howland (Clift) are outsiders because of their rugged individualism; the airplane pilot Guido (Wallach) has been adrift since the death of his wife. Together, they capture beautiful wild mustangs, which they sell to a manufacturer of dog food.

Despite the presence of three strong male leads, the focus of the film is Marilyn's character, Roslyn Tabor. Roslyn's sensitivity and ethereal beauty draw each of the men to her. Though supposedly friends, the men cannot relate to each other. They relate only to Roslyn, for she represents something each of them needs or desires. Each man bares his heart to her, and each has his own theory about what makes her special. Roslyn herself feels isolated from society, at least temporarily, because she has come to Reno for a divorce. Reno, the divorce capital of the world, provides the perfect setting for a story of alienation.

Let's Make Love *perks up only in isolated moments, most notably in Marilyn's lively "My Heart Belongs to Daddy" number. All told, the film slowed the forward momentum of Marilyn's career.*

Roslyn forces the men to confront their barren existences when she pleads with them not to kill the wild mustangs they have worked so hard to round up. But the three believe that their occupation gives them a freedom that is better than the slavery of working for "wages." Paradoxically, it is this "freedom" that keeps them isolated from society and alienated from other human beings. Their steadfast adherence to their brand of independence is both their strength and their weakness.

Like the cowboys, the wild horses are the last of a vanishing breed—a parallel that eludes the three men. By killing off the horses, the cowboys are destroying the last vestiges of the lifestyle they so desperately cling to. In killing the horses, they are essentially killing themselves.

In the end, Roslyn wins. The horses are set free, and she and Gay ride off together toward "that big star straight on," which will take them "right home." Despite the lack of any concrete solutions to the characters' personal dilemmas, the film's ending is a positive one.

Arthur Miller wrote the screenplay for The Misfits as a tribute to his wife. Pictured with Marilyn are (from left) producer Frank Taylor, Montgomery Clift, Eli Wallach, Miller, director John Huston, and Clark Gable.

Not surprisingly, *The Misfits* is closely identified with Miller and Monroe, yet a story involving a group of characters who embark on a doomed quest is typical of director John Huston's output, as well. In Huston's films, the hero is often an obsessed professional who risks everything for the quest, just as Gay dedicates himself so passionately to capturing the wild mustangs. Huston's female characters generally disrupt the quest, or otherwise tempt the hero into losing sight of his goals. So it is that Huston's women are generally destructive characters. In *The Misfits*, however, Roslyn is a positive force, and her disruption of the cowboys' goal to sell mustangs for dog food becomes an affirmation of life.

Marilyn and her intense costar, Montgomery Clift.

The shoot of *The Misfits* was a tortuous one. Away from her psychiatrist and emotionally estranged from Miller, Marilyn increased her prescription-drug intake considerably, a situation made more dangerous by her drinking. Her despair during the first few weeks of production darkened until it seemed as though she would be swallowed up completely. Miller had hoped that *The Misfits* would bring Marilyn back to him, but he quickly realized that "if there was a key to Marilyn's despair I did not possess it."

Marilyn had idolized Clark Gable since her childhood. The opportunity to play opposite the gentlemanly legend was a dream come true for the troubled actress.

Marilyn grew increasingly bitter toward Miller, directing all of her hostility and frustration at him, though he did little to warrant such treatment. Marilyn felt betrayed by her marriage, perhaps because it did not meet her high expectations for happiness. And once Marilyn felt betrayed, she exiled all involved parties from her life. Looking for excuses to expel Miller, she lashed out at his sceenplay for *The Misfits*, complaining, "He could have written me anything, and he comes up with this. If that's what he thinks of me, well, then, I'm not for him and he's not for me."

Near the end of August, Marilyn suffered a breakdown and was evacuated to Westside Hospital in Los Angeles. As the mercury in Nevada topped 100 degrees, her pale body was wrapped in a wet sheet and carried into a plane for the flight west. Under the care of her psychiatrist and her internist, Marilyn stayed in the hospital ten days while production was shut down. In apparent affirmation that Marilyn's precarious health was by then public knowledge, columnist Louella Parsons reported that the star was "a very sick girl, much sicker than at first believed." Marilyn returned to the set the following week, though production would be halted periodically throughout September because of Marilyn's problems.

Marilyn and Montgomery Clift: two lost souls.

Marilyn's emotional distress during the filming of The Misfits *was problem enough, but an added obstacle was the unbearably hot Nevada weather. Marilyn finally collapsed and was flown to Westside Hospital in Los Angeles, where she remained for ten days.*

Aside from the tenuousness of Marilyn's mental and emotional state, the production labored beneath the shadows of other potential disasters. Montgomery Clift, a self-destructive soul who had disfigured his handsome looks by accidentally driving his car into a telephone pole in 1957, was as dependent on alcohol and drugs as Marilyn, prompting the sensitive actress to exclaim, "He's the only person I know who's in worse shape than I am." His reputation was such that insurance companies would no longer underwrite Clift in a film. However, because of the efforts of Miller, Huston, and powerful Hollywood executive Lew Wasserman, insurance on the tragic actor finally came through. Despite his dubious reputation and his excessive drinking on the set, Clift never missed a day of work and had learned his entire part before shooting began. Yet, at the time, his participation was a source of considerable anxiety. Following *The Misfits*, Clift would make only three more films before succumbing to coronary artery disease in 1966.

The viewer of The Misfits *inevitably wonders what proportion of Marilyn's
performance simply reflects the turmoil that was going on inside of her.
But by any standard, her performance is ambitious and thoroughly convincing.
Gable, too, handled his role with subtlety and conviction.*

Other on-set problems included Paula Strasberg's almost total monopoly of Marilyn. The two spent a great deal of time together on and off the set. They exhaustively discussed lines, strategy, and characterization, usually while sequestered in Marilyn's air-conditioned limousine. At one point, Marilyn moved out of the hotel suite she shared with Miller and into Strasberg's. Huston's style of direction, in which he trusted the actors' contribution to characterization, allowed Strasberg a great deal of leeway in terms of her influence on Marilyn. Yet, Huston did not respect Strasberg and would not let her interfere with his direction.

Clark Gable's participation in *The Misfits* must have seemed to Marilyn like a gift from the gods. Her adulation of Gable went all the way back to her childhood, when she had fantasized that the handsome actor was her father. Her presumed real father, C. Stanley Gifford, is said to have resembled Gable—at least as much as any mere mortal could. In 1947, Marilyn took singing and acting lessons from actor John Carroll, who was considered a Gable lookalike. Finally, in 1954, at a party thrown in her honor, Marilyn was able to meet the King of Hollywood. They dined, danced, and cheerfully discussed making a film together someday. She was thrilled when Gable agreed in 1958 to take the lead role of Gay Langland in *The Misfits*.

Just as Marilyn had always dreamed, Gable proved to be not just a consummate professional, but a strong, sensitive gentleman. As the grueling location shoot of *The Misfits* was made more unbearable by the long waits for Marilyn, Gable showed no anger or hostility toward the obviously ill actress. On the set, Marilyn claimed, "The place was full of so-called men, but Clark was the one who brought a chair for me between the takes." According to his agent, Charles Chasin, the legendary movie star realized that *The Misfits* was one of the best of his 70 films. Yet privately Gable admitted his frustration with Marilyn's behavior and hinted at his growing fatigue from his participation in the film.

Even nature seemed intent on complicating production of *The Misfits*— Reno's summer temperatures often reached an excrutiating 108 degrees. With several cast members in various states of deteriorating health, the climate itself became an enemy.

The Misfits is a thoughtful, deeply reflective film. Yet for all its interest in the disappointments and compromises that define the characters' lives . . .

. . . it also reveals the bright, healing potential of the human spirit. With this film, Marilyn moved beyond mere "sex symbol" status, and became a symbol of life itself.

The Misfits is not jolly entertainment, but then, it never set out to be. In retrospect, the film can be regarded as a dignified and meaningful conclusion to the careers of two of Hollywood's truly imperishable personalities.

Despite these obstacles, and despite Marilyn's dependency on drugs and alcohol, Huston obtained a remarkable performance from his star. Though some biographers accuse Marilyn of walking through the role in a state of suspended animation, their assessments are unfair ones, grounded in hindsight and based on the sensationalized anecdotes about her substance abuse. In truth, Marilyn's performance is credible and forceful, and owes much to her Method training, which allowed her to immerse herself totally in the role of Roslyn. In addition, Miller's effective blending of the real-life Marilyn Monroe with the fictional Roslyn helped Marilyn's characterization, as did Huston's directorial approach, in which the actors were given leeway to explore their characters.

Huston had had a long-standing respect for Marilyn, and retained it, despite the exasperation of directing *The Misfits*. He blamed her troubles on doctors who gave her too much medication, as well as on the studios that condoned it. In a 1981 interview, Huston declared Marilyn to be a fine actress, "not an actress in the technical sense, but . . . she had that ability to go down within herself and pull up an emotion and give it." But for all of Marilyn's efforts and the good work of the other people connected with the film, *The Misfits* opened to mixed reviews and poor box-office results—neither a fair nor fitting end to Marilyn's remarkable career.

By the end of *The Misfits* shoot, Marilyn's marriage to Arthur Miller was effectively over. After the film wrapped in early November, the two left for New York in separate planes. On November 11, she officially announced their separation to columnist Earl Wilson. The press swarmed her New York residence and a tearful Marilyn emerged to confirm the story. According to one Monroe biographer, newsmen were so eager to get to her that one reporter shoved his microphone into her mouth, chipping one of her teeth in the process.

Marilyn attempted to go into seclusion, but her efforts were thwarted by the announcement of Clark Gable's death on November 16. Gable had had a massive heart attack the day after *The Misfits* had wrapped, but many had believed he was improving. His sudden death was a severe blow. Marilyn took the news so badly that she was unable to make a coherent statement to the press, who kept calling for her comments. Finally, she managed a brief statement: "This is a great shock to me. I'm deeply sorry. Clark Gable was one of the finest men I ever met. He was one of the most decent human.

Rumors began flying that Kay Gable, Clark's young widow who was pregnant with his first child, blamed Marilyn for her husband's death. Kay claimed that the stress Gable had had to endure during the filming of *The Misfits*, including the daily delays in excessive heat, had led to his heart attack. Upon hearing this, Marilyn spiraled into a dark depression—the thought that she had caused the death of the man she had idolized since childhood was too much to bear. The following May, Kay Gable would invite Marilyn to the christening of Gable's son, John Clark Gable. A grateful Marilyn took the invitation as a sign that Kay no longer held her responsible for any part in her husband's death.

As the winter of 1960-61 deepened, so did Marilyn's feelings of despair and hopelessness. Christmas without Miller or Montand underscored her loneliness, though Joe DiMaggio entered her life once more and renewed their relationship. A close friendship developed between the former husband and wife and the press spread rumors of a possible reconciliation. In January, Marilyn flew to Mexico for a quick divorce from Arthur Miller, and then drew up a new will. She made her half-sister Berniece Miracle a major beneficiary, though she had seen Miracle only a few times during her life. She also made provisions for the care of her mother, and left money to various friends as well as to her secretary, May Reis. She gave Lee Strasberg and one of her psychiatrists, Dr. Marianne Kris, portions of her estate and also left Strasberg all of her personal effects and clothing. Sadly, the will is the document of a woman with only the thinnest shred of a family and just a few friends. Most of the latter were not close personal friends, but colleagues, employees, or doctors—those who had some financial or industry relationship with Marilyn.

In 1960 photographer Eve Arnold discovered that Marilyn's troubles had not diminished her capacity for seduction.

Joe DiMaggio re-entered Marilyn's life during the cheerless period that followed The Misfits. *Here, the couple enjoys a ballgame at Yankee Stadium in 1961.*

In February of 1961, Marilyn entered the Payne-Whitney Clinic in New York at the suggestion of her East Coast psychiatrist, Dr. Kris. From the start, Marilyn was not comfortable at Payne-Whitney. Surprised at the security precautions, which included barred windows and glass panes in the door so that nurses could glance inside, she rebelled at being treated "like a nut." She felt that the employees at the clinic were checking on her more often than on the other patients because she was a movie star. She was allowed a limited number of phone calls, which she used to reach Joe DiMaggio in Florida. DiMaggio returned to New York, arranged Marilyn's discharge from Payne-Whitney, and placed her in Columbia-Presbyterian Medical Center. Upon her release from Columbia three weeks later, reporters and photographers disgraced themselves in an insensitive display outside the hospital's doors. They surrounded Marilyn, screaming tasteless questions and blocking her exit to a waiting limousine. Sixteen police officers and hospital security men were needed to get her safely to her car. She spent part of the next month in Florida with DiMaggio, who continued to look after her as much as she would allow until her death.

By 1961, Marilyn's visits to hospitals had become almost routine. In February of that year she underwent psychiatric treatment at the Payne-Whitney Clinic in New York. Later in the month she was transferred to Columbia Presbyterian Medical Center. On March 5, she was released . . .

. . . and had to face the usual throng of reporters and fans. Marilyn's "private" life was by this time almost nonexistent.

In addition to her precarious emotional and mental health, Marilyn experienced a variety of physical disorders as well. In May 1961, she entered Cedars of Lebanon Hospital in Los Angeles for gynecological surgery. The following month, she found herself in the Polyclinic Hospital of New York for a gallbladder operation. In addition, Marilyn suffered from an ulcerated colon and abnormal bleeding from the uterus. Because of her delicate mental and physical conditions, Marilyn did not work as an actress at all in 1961.

Sometime after her split with Arthur Miller, Marilyn began dating Frank Sinatra and became an unofficial member of Sinatra's "Rat Pack," that group of show-business cronies with whom the legendary singer maintained close personal and professional ties. Core members of the Rat Pack included Dean Martin, Sammy Davis, Jr., Peter Lawford, and Joey Bishop. Marilyn had known Sinatra for many years, and some biographers speculate that the two may have enjoyed a relationship years earlier, though no hard evidence exists to support this. Their friendship was probably renewed during the shooting of *The Misfits*, when Marilyn was flown to Los Angeles after her breakdown. Supposedly, Sinatra called to inquire about her health and wish her well. Earlier, he had invited the cast of *The Misfits* to watch him perform at the Cal-Neva Lodge. Sinatra was in the process of purchasing the lodge, which was located near Lake Tahoe, directly on the border of California and Nevada. Marilyn would visit the lodge several times over the remaining two years of her life. (The singer would later sell the business, when his link with organized crime was leaked to the press and the public.) Sinatra gave Marilyn a small white poodle to replace the dog she lost in the divorce with Miller. Marilyn, who always had a spirited sense of humor, called the dog "Maf," which was short for Mafia.

March 7, 1961, following the funeral of Marilyn's former mother-in-law, Augusta Miller. Marilyn once said of Augusta, "She opened her heart to me."

Emotionally adrift, Marilyn socialized with the "Rat Pack," whose members included (from left) Frank Sinatra, Sammy Davis, Jr., and Peter Lawford.

Marilyn had known actor Peter Lawford since her starlet days, when he had escorted her to a few Hollywood functions. Her association with both Sinatra and Lawford undoubtedly brought her into contact with John Kennedy, perhaps as early as July of 1960, when the young senator clinched the Democratic nomination for president. At the time, Lawford was married to Pat Kennedy, JFK's younger sister. According to some accounts, Marilyn was one of those in attendance at the L.A. Coliseum when John Kennedy made his acceptance speech, and she appeared at the celebration bash at Romanoff's restaurant afterward. There she was introduced to the next President of the United States.

However, a few biographers maintain that she had met Kennedy as far back as 1951, when the two had attended a couple of parties in Los Angeles thrown by agent Charles Feldman; such claims are not substantiated by hard evidence or credible eyewitness accounts. Lawford's third wife, Deborah Gould, has stated that Kennedy first met Marilyn during the 1960 presidential campaign but that the meeting occurred a few months prior to Kennedy's July nomination. Whatever the case, it is generally accepted that Marilyn Monroe and John Kennedy were engaged in a love affair throughout 1961, if not earlier. A November 1960 column by Art Buchwald supports these theories. Titled "Let's Be Firm on Monroe Doctrine," the item read, "Who will be the next ambassador to Monroe? This is one of the many problems President-elect Kennedy will have to work on in January. Obviously you can't leave Monroe adrift. There are too many greedy people eyeing her, and now that Ambassador Miller has left she could flounder around without any direction."

Between her failing mental and physical health, her trips back and forth from Los Angeles to New York, and her continued abuse of drugs and alcohol, Marilyn Monroe led a fruitless existence during the year or so after the completion of *The Misfits*. During the latter half of 1961, she settled into an apartment on Doheny Drive in Beverly Hills. She began to see just one psychiatrist at this time, Dr. Ralph Greenson. Greenson took great pains with Marilyn and opened up his home to her—an unusual interpretation of the doctor-patient relationship. She visited the Greenson family on a regular basis and became quite friendly with the psychiatrist's daughter, Joan. Marilyn even spent Christmas with the Greensons that year. When the doctor suggested that Marilyn hire his friend Eunice Murray as her housekeeper, Marilyn readily agreed.

The precise circumstances of Marilyn's relationship with John F. Kennedy are unclear, but it is likely that the pair had a love affair in 1960-61, and possibly earlier. Apropos of JFK, Marilyn allegedly remarked, "I think I make his back feel better."

As 1962 began, Greenson suggested that Marilyn look for a house of her own—something that he hoped would bring her some sense of security. Despite her fame and fortune, Marilyn had never owned a house by herself. With the help of Eunice Murray, Marilyn found a home she liked in the Brentwood area of Los Angeles. The single-story, Mexican-style house was attractive but modest. A tile with a coat of arms and a Latin inscription was planted just outside the front door. The inscription read, "Cursum Perficio," or, "I am finishing my journey." Marilyn had less than six months to live.

Marilyn's February 1962 purchase of her new home, and her winning of a Golden Globe Award as the "world's film favorite" in March, would be the last two high points of her life. According to some accounts, Greenson had been able to minimize Marilyn's drug intake for a short time, but she quickly began to slide back into old habits as disappointments mounted and the future seemed too painful to face.

In April, Marilyn returned to Twentieth Century-Fox to begin production on *Something's Got to Give*, an updated version of a 1940 comedy hit entitled *My Favorite Wife*. George Cukor was set to direct. From the start, Marilyn disliked the Nunally Johnson-Walter Bernstein script, which was not yet finalized when shooting began. By 1962, the chief production executive at Fox was Peter Levathes, a onetime advertising executive known for his hostility toward actors. He had just come through some monumental problems during the production of *Cleopatra*, and was faced with crippling cost overruns because of that film. To say there were tensions on the set of *Something's Got to Give* is a gross understatement.

Marilyn hugs the Golden Globe award she received in early 1962; with her is Rock Hudson.

Marilyn's unfinished final project,
Something's Got to Give, *included a role for her friend Wally Cox.*

Marilyn reported to work at Fox for hair, makeup, and costume tests, though neither Dr. Greenson nor Marilyn's internist felt she should undertake the production of a new film. She had contracted a virus that spring, which left her fatigued and weakened. Realizing that Marilyn was ill, the studio executives, Cukor, and costar Dean Martin agreed to arrange the shooting schedule around her. Despite this consideration, Marilyn showed up for work only six days during the month of May.

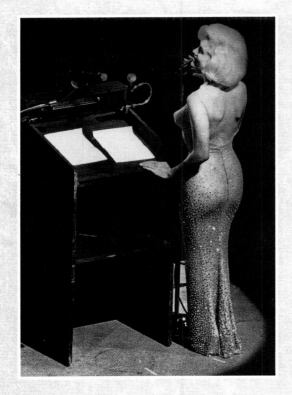

Marilyn wowed 'em at Madison Square Garden when she warbled "Happy Birthday" to President Kennedy.

Toward the end of May, Marilyn made a quick trip to New York. Peter Lawford had asked her to sing "Happy Birthday" at a massive birthday celebration for President Kennedy at Madison Square Garden. Despite her virus and her film commitment, Marilyn heartily agreed to go. Arthur Miller's father, Isidore, escorted his former daughter-in-law to the party, where she sang her breathy and notoriously suggestive version of "Happy Birthday" to Kennedy. Marilyn's performance and Kennedy's subsequent quip ("I can now retire from politics after having 'Happy Birthday' sung to me in such a sweet, wholesome way.") are chilling in light of the later revelations about their affair, and what fate had in store for JFK. The event is made more ironic by Lawford's opening remarks, in which he referred to the tardy actress as "the late Marilyn Monroe."

The Fox executives were livid with Marilyn for appearing at the Kennedy bash in New York. If she was too sick to show up for work, then she should have been too sick to fly across the country for a personal appearance. The event signaled a turning point in Fox's treatment of Marilyn; henceforth, they would take a hard line.

Photographers on the set of Something's Got to Give *got an eyeful when Marilyn took a dip in the altogether.*

Marilyn showed up for work more frequently over the next two weeks. In production at that time was a swimming pool sequence in which Marilyn was supposed to wear a flesh-colored bathing suit to suggest that she was swimming nude. Possibly because of the titillating nature of the scene, several photographers had been invited to shoot publicity stills. The photographers got an added bonus that night because Marilyn immediately shucked her suit and paddled around *au naturel.* Newsreel and still lensmen scampered to capture the famous "nude swim," during which a carefree Marilyn playfully teased the photographers with glimpses of her naked body. Her true love—the camera—remained faithful to the end, and Marilyn did not disappoint.

On June 1, Marilyn turned 36 years old, and the cast and crew surprised her with a small birthday celebration on the set. It was also her last day of work. Out of 33 shooting days, Marilyn had showed up on the set only 12 times. Often hours late when she did appear, she seldom got through more than one script page per day—at least according to a studio statement released to the press. On June 8, 1962, production chief Peter Levathes fired Marilyn from *Something's Got to Give*. Plans were made to replace Marilyn with Lee Remick, who said at the time, "I don't know whether to feel sorry for [Marilyn] or not. I feel she should have been replaced. The movie business is crumbling down around our ears because of that kind of behavior. Actors shouldn't be allowed to get away with that kind of thing."

Marilyn was devastated by her dismissal and considered it a personal rejection. Dean Martin, perhaps out of friendship or loyalty to Marilyn, refused to continue the film with Remick. (The picture was eventually reworked as a vehicle for Doris Day and James Garner, and released in 1963 as *Move Over, Darling*.) Besides still photographs, all that remains of *Something's Got to Give* are snippets of Marilyn's wardrobe tests and a few scenes, including the swimming pool sequence. In this footage, Marilyn looks more beautiful than ever before; lithe and trim, her hair a soft, pure platinum, she seems more a creature of light and air than one of flesh. The public saw this footage for the first time in *Marilyn*, a 1963 Fox compilation film hosted by Rock Hudson.

Marilyn's nude swim delighted photographers and certainly intrigued the public, but did not move Something's Got to Give *any closer to completion. Shortly afterward, Marilyn was fired by Fox. She would never again work on a movie set.*

Playful and spirited, Marilyn seemed to have banished her demons.

Marilyn's dismissal from *Something's Got to Give* coincided with a wildly chaotic lifestyle: She dated several men, took dangerous quantities of sleeping pills, and relied on daily visits to Dr. Greenson to see her through each 24-hour period. It is widely alleged that, sometime during 1962, Marilyn began a relationship with John Kennedy's very married brother, Robert. The younger Kennedy not only served as Attorney General for the President, but it also seems that he eased Marilyn Monroe out of his older brother's life. Reportedly, JFK's advisers felt that his affair with Marilyn was politically dangerous and encouraged him to break it off.

Speculation on Marilyn's affair with Robert Kennedy is based on numerous eyewitness reports of their meetings together, particularly at Peter Lawford's beachfront home in Malibu. However, specific facts regarding their relationship are even more scarce than those involving Marilyn and JFK. Details conflict and versions of the same anecdotes are contradictory. Some biographers maintain that Marilyn met RFK at one of Lawford's dinner parties in 1961, while others suggest she was introduced to him at the New York birthday bash in May 1962. What does remain difficult to discount is that Marilyn made repeated phone calls to the Justice Department—where Attorney General Robert Kennedy worked—shortly after she was fired by Fox.

Did Marilyn have an affair with the very married Robert Kennedy? RFK wasn't telling.

At this point, the speculation takes a decidedly unbelievable turn. In the summer of 1962, Robert Kennedy and/or his advisers supposedly concluded that his involvement with Marilyn—like his brother's—was potentially dangerous. Their decision was based not only on Marilyn's perilous mental state but also on the knowledge that organized crime figures were determined to ruin RFK. As Attorney General, Kennedy had gone after such top mobsters as Sam Giancana and such Mafia-connected union leaders as Jimmy Hoffa. Both of these men vowed publicly and privately to destroy the younger Kennedy. Some evidence suggests that Marilyn's house was bugged in the weeks before her death, and that the actress herself knew about it. Many have speculated that certain organized crime leaders—eager to catch Robert Kennedy literally with his pants down—were responsible for the wiretaps in Marilyn's home. Whatever the true facts, RFK apparently called off the relationship a short time after Marilyn's dismissal from Fox.

The last few days of Marilyn's life have been detailed many times in often-contradictory accounts. Desperate attempts to reach Robert Kennedy by phone are coupled with news that Twentieth Century-Fox may call her back to complete *Something's Got to Give*; rumors of her endlessly drugged state are mingled with discussions about her plans to decorate her new home; reports of her lack of interest in her physical appearance are belied by the personal satisfaction she felt in Bert Stern's photographic session with her in July.

On August 4, 1962, Marilyn spent the morning talking with her publicist, Pat Newcomb, and the rest of the day making phone calls to her friends. Dr. Greenson visited her for a short time in the early evening. The number of people who claim to have talked with Marilyn on her last day is phenomenal— everyone from Joe DiMaggio, Jr. to Marlon Brando, from Sidney Skolsky to Isidore Miller. From her bedroom, Marilyn continued to make phone calls into the night. With each call, her speech became more slurred, a reaction that was not unusual for her during this period of heavy sedative use. Apparently, none of her friends were sufficiently alarmed to have someone check on her. Supposedly, Marilyn called Peter Lawford that evening to say goodbye. Then, sometime during the night of August 4-5, 1962, Marilyn Monroe died alone, her white phone still clutched in her hand.

Marilyn's death stunned the world.

Just as the press had hounded Marilyn in life, so they descended upon her in death, photographing her blanketed body as it was moved out of the house, into the ambulance, and away to the morgue. Pat Newcomb lashed out at the reporters for their lack of sensitivity, calling them "vultures." The publicist may not have been too far off the mark, for one reporter was heard to say, "I'm just as sorry as the next fellow about Marilyn Monroe. But as long as she had to do it, what a break that she did it in August."

*The toy dogs Marilyn left behind observe a
visit from the police.*

Marilyn's death was ruled a "probable suicide." Her funeral took place on August 8, at the Westwood Memorial Park Chapel in Westwood, California. Arrangements were made by Joe DiMaggio, with the help of Marilyn's half-sister, Berniece Miracle, and Marilyn's business manager, Inez Melson. The services were conducted by Rev. A.J. Soldan, who read the 23rd Psalm, the 14th chapter of the Book of John, and excerpts from the 46th and 139th Psalms. Lee Strasberg delivered a short eulogy, and Judy Garland's "Over the Rainbow" was selected as the music. DiMaggio allowed only a few people to attend the funeral; Marilyn's most recent Hollywood acquaintances were noticeably absent.

Almost immediately, newspapers published rumors involving inconsistencies in accounts of Marilyn's death. An article in the *Los Angeles Herald-Examiner* related unsubstantiated stories about her body being secretly moved from its place in the morgue. Another article in the same paper reported on the considerable gaps in the timetable of events from the fateful evening. Friends and colleagues interviewed at the time seemed torn over whether Marilyn had committed suicide or succumbed to an accidental overdose of sleeping pills.

Marilyn's fame was worldwide, of course, and her death was widely covered by the British press.

At Marilyn's funeral, a grief-stricken Joe DiMaggio bent over Marilyn's casket and whispered, "I love you." He was accompanied to the services by his son, Joe, Jr.

Over the years, various self-styled "investigators" have claimed that members of organized crime killed Marilyn to frame the Kennedys, or that the CIA killed her to discredit the Kennedy administration, or that the Kennedys themselves killed her to avoid public scandal. None of the proponents of these theories have uncovered enough evidence to make a credible newspaper story, let alone a legal case. For all of the hints of mystery surrounding Marilyn's death, the official investigators never felt a need to pursue the case beyond a superficial level. More than likely, there was no crime, only the covering up of unwise relationships. Some doubt that there was even a suicide, speculating that, on the last night of her life, Marilyn had wanted merely to sleep through her despair, as she had done so many times before. Her mind fuzzied, she simply lost track of the number of sleeping pills she had swallowed.

Perhaps in trying to come to grips with the tragic struggle of Marilyn's life, we have become obsessed with explaining her death. No matter, for any attempt to unmask the truth about her last hours remains futile. Marilyn Monroe took her secrets with her.

Berniece Baker Miracle, Marilyn's half-sister, arrives at Westwood Memorial Park.

At peace.

The desolate expression on the face of Paula Strasberg (with husband Lee) conveys the awful reality: Marilyn was gone.

LEGEND

". . . it's nice, people knowing who you are and all of that,
and feeling that you've meant something to them."

MARILYN MONROE

So great has been Marilyn's popularity that her legend took root during her lifetime. This striking 1954 painting by abstract expressionist Willem de Kooning celebrates Marilyn's vibrant, energizing appeal.

Just days after Marilyn's death, these youngsters visited her handprints at Grauman's Chinese Theater. Since then, innumerable devotees have made the pilgrimage.

*I*t would be an injustice to Marilyn Monroe to end her story with an account of her tragic death, for in many ways, she is very much alive. Her stardom has not only survived the last three decades, it has escalated. Some maintain that Marilyn has more fans in death than she did in life—a claim substantiated by the large number of fan clubs based all over the world, the renewed popularity of her films as a result of their release on video, and her identity as an icon of American pop culture.

Even during her lifetime, Marilyn reached a level of popularity that surpassed that of many of her peers. Her power as a star was indicated by the box-office success of her films, by the groundbreaking contract she negotiated with her studio, and by the amount of publicity she generated in the press. She also inspired many imitators in her lifetime. It is this phenomenon, in particular, that speaks volumes about her popularity. Her success inspired rival film studios to groom buxom blondes the way horticulturists grow flowers. Seemingly overnight there appeared a crop of beauties who emulated Marilyn's physical appearance in bids to become "the next Marilyn Monroe." Some of these starlets were talented and inspired followings of their own. Others, who simply copied Marilyn's hair or provocative voice, quickly dropped out of sight.

Jayne Mansfield joined Marilyn as a Twentieth Century-Fox contract player in the 1950s. Though a clever comedienne and a shrewd self-promoter, Mansfield lived forever in Marilyn's shadow. From the moment Jayne burst onto the scene in the Broadway version of *Will Success Spoil Rock Hunter?*, she was compared, contrasted, and sometimes even equated with the world's most famous blonde. Like Marilyn, she had a burning ambition to become a movie star, and she labored to build her own image through outrageous publicity stunts. Unlike other copycat Monroes, Mansfield was a spirited performer with a flair for broad comedy. However, what little success she did enjoy was garnered through roles in which she parodied Marilyn Monroe. In a business that thrives on image and typecasting, Mansfield's chances of escaping the inevitable comparisons to Marilyn were next to impossible. Despite early Hollywood triumphs like *The Girl Can't Help It* and the film version of *Rock Hunter*, Mansfield's gifts were eventually perceived as limited, and her career quickly fell to pieces after 1960.

The actress Jayne Mansfield had replaced as Fox's "second dizzy blonde" was Sheree North. North was a talented and dynamic dancer, but the studio used her only as a pawn in its attempts to keep Marilyn in line. When Marilyn refused to do *How to Be Very, Very Popular* and *The Girl in Pink Tights*, Fox threatened to replace her with North. Eventually, adorned with hair and makeup designed by the studio to resemble Marilyn's, North did star in *How to Be Very, Very Popular*. The role was tailored to fit Marilyn's image instead of to suit North's undeniable talents, and the picture was not the box-office success the studio had hoped for. Shortly after Mansfield's arrival at Fox, North disappeared from the big screen and did not return for almost a decade.

Other film studios promoted their own versions of Marilyn Monroe, though none of these challengers matched the original's unique combination of wit, native intelligence, and sensual beauty. Pouty Mamie Van Doren starred in such B-movie cult classics as *High School Confidential!* and *Untamed Youth*, and served as Universal Pictures' sexy siren throughout the late 1950s. Van Doren managed to snag a showy supporting role in *Teacher's Pet*, a major production that starred Clark Gable and Doris Day, but was mainly relegated to starring roles in exploitation pictures.

Of all the Hollywood blondes who patterned themselves after Marilyn, Jayne Mansfield enjoyed the most success. But nonstop self-promotion took its toll, and Mansfield descended into caricature.

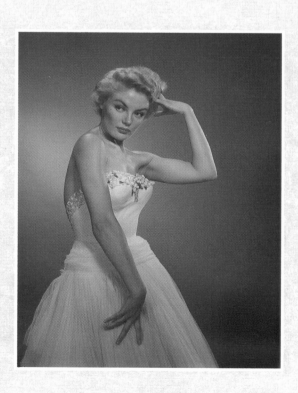

Ill-used by Twentieth Century-Fox in the 1950s, talented Sheree North eventually made her mark as a dependable character actress.

Universal Pictures touted Mamie Van Doren as "the girl built like a platinum powerhouse," but her career stalled in B-movies. Years later, curvy and good-humored in middle age, she achieved cult status.

Many of the copycat Monroes exaggerated the sexual side of Marilyn's image—an approach that doomed them to one-dimensional roles as sexpots and sex objects. Generally, their careers followed a pattern of early affiliation with a particular studio, followed by freelance assignments in increasingly unappetizing productions. This lower-echelon group of Marilyn imitators includes MGM's Joi Lansing, Columbia's Beverly Michaels and Cleo Moore, and RKO's Diana Dors. Provocative though they were, these MM acolytes never progressed beyond bit parts in major films, or starring roles in such B-movie favorites as *The Atomic Submarine*, *Blonde Bait*, *One Girl's Confession*, and *Blonde Sinner*, respectively.

English actress Diana Dors began her film career as a teenager in 1946, and later lightened her hair to become Britain's "answer" to Marilyn. By the late 1960s, she was playing plumply attractive matrons.

The statuesque Anita Ekberg.

Pretty Joi Lansing had been a teenage model before entering films in 1948. She is probably best-known for her recurring role as the gorgeous model pursued by photographer Bob Cummings on TV's Love That Bob.

Perhaps the closest to Marilyn's physical presence and bold sensuality was Swedish actress Anita Ekberg, though Ekberg lacked Marilyn's touch of innocence and flair for comedy. She also chose a different path than Marilyn, appearing in mostly European films—including Federico Fellini's *La Dolce Vita*—after 1958.

That Marilyn's popularity was immense during her lifetime is understandable, but the escalation of her fame since her death is considered nothing short of a phenomenon, and has been a continual source of fascination to biographers, cultural critics, and her fans.

Undoubtedly, part of our unending interest in Marilyn is due to her premature death and the mysterious circumstances surrounding it. Occasional efforts are made to persuade the Los Angeles police to reopen her case. At such times, speculation and rumor run rampant as a few more bits and pieces of information come to light. In 1974, Robert Slatzer, a onetime friend to Marilyn who claims to have married her in 1953, authored a book alleging that the famous star had been murdered. Entitled *The Life and Curious Death of Marilyn Monroe*, the book cites her relationship with both Kennedys, probes into the questions surrounding her death, and comes up with a provocative—but ultimately unconvincing—murder theory.

Slatzer hired a private detective named Milo Speriglio to obtain hard evidence to support his theory. Speriglio has devoted more than 15 years to the case and claims to know who murdered Marilyn and why, though he can't prove it. In 1982, he offered a reward of $10,000 for Marilyn's so-called "red diary," which the detective claims details her conversations with Robert Kennedy. Supposedly, Slatzer saw the diary a few days before Marilyn died, while coroner's aide Lionel Grandison noticed it in the coroner's room. Interestingly, Speriglio's announcement about the diary coincided with the publication of his first book, *Marilyn Monroe: Murder Cover-Up*, which recaps Slatzer's book and brings the investigation up to date. Later that year, a collector of rare books offered $150,000 for the diary, which has yet to surface; many people doubt its existence altogether.

In 1986, Speriglio wrote a second book on the Monroe case, *The Marilyn Conspiracy*, which is an updated version of his earlier work. That same year, Speriglio called a press conference to demand that the case be reopened. His request was denied.

Though many doubt the veracity of Slatzer and Speriglio's theories and conclusions, the rumors of a murder or a cover-up serve to keep Marilyn's name in the news, as do the tributes and retrospectives that surface on the anniversary of her death. The murder rumors add a tone of notoriety to her story, while the tributes and accolades remind us that there was much more to her than love affairs and an unexplained death. Both types of publicity tend to escalate her myth, assigning her a permanent place in the annals of Hollywood folklore.

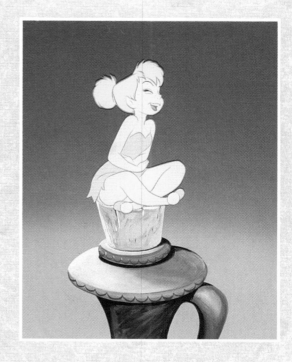

Of all the ways that Marilyn's legend has been interpreted, few are as unusual—or as charming—as the Tinker Bell character in Walt Disney's cartoon version of Peter Pan. *Stage productions and a silent-film version of the famous play had depicted Tinker Bell as a beam of light, but Disney wanted the sprite to have a human appearance. His animators complied by modeling Tinker on Hollywood's most famous blonde.*

It is the job of biographers to sort out fact from folklore and to analyze Marilyn Monroe's significance to our culture. Some biographers take to the task quite readily, while others miss the mark, adding to the mountain of misinformation already in existence. The best biographies are by authors who have thoroughly researched her life by interviewing former associates and friends, reviewing original publicity articles and news accounts, and assessing the effects of certain films and photographs on her career. *Legend: The Life and Death of Marilyn Monroe* by Fred Lawrence Guiles and *Goddess: The Secret Lives of Marilyn Monroe* by Anthony Summers offer the most detailed and straightforward biographies. Though some estimates claim that more than 300 books about Marilyn Monroe have been written, very few accounts of her life were authored before she died. The best of these remains Maurice Zolotow's *Marilyn Monroe*, first published in 1960. Sometimes a picture is truly worth a thousand words; *Monroe: Her Life in Pictures* by James Spada with George Zeno, *Marilyn: An Appreciation* by Eve Arnold, and *Marilyn Monroe and the Camera* chronicle the actress's career with a selection of poignant and provocative photographs.

Most suspect of all publications on Marilyn Monroe are personal accounts by acquaintances who knew her only slightly or as employees, and tell-all stories by male associates who claim to have had a physical relationship with her. (If all those who claimed to have been one of Marilyn's lovers are telling the truth, then she would hardly have had time to make any films!)

A great deal of Marilyn's singing has been preserved on records, some of which are collectible picture discs.

Marilyn has inspired countless books and magazines. Many are beautiful, and are treasured by collectors.

As a cultural figure, Marilyn Monroe has inspired important authors and playwrights to analyze her life and career, and her impact on our society. Two interesting—and contradictory—points of view are offered by Norman Mailer and Gloria Steinem in their respective books. Despite the title, Mailer's *Marilyn: A Biography* is not a factual, straightforward account of her life. Instead, the Pulitzer Prize-winning author took the bare outline of the actress's life and career and filled it in with his impressions, creating what he called a "novel biography." He hypothesizes about what Marilyn thought of certain events, and interprets her feelings about the people in her life. In the end, Mailer tells us more about Marilyn Monroe's effect on the men of his generation than he does about the actress herself.

In contrast to Mailer's male-oriented interpretation is the feminist perspective of Gloria Steinem's *Marilyn: Norma Jeane*, composed of a series of essays on topics related to the star's life and image. Steinem approaches her subject insightfully, and with a unique point of view that became possible only after the advent of the women's movement. The forces that affected Marilyn's life and career are reinterpreted through a woman's eyes. Though one might expect Steinem to be critical of Marilyn's sex-symbol persona, the feminist empathizes with the actress's struggle for success and respect. Steinem's approach emphasizes Marilyn's humanity by downplaying her sexuality.

Underappreciated as a singer in her lifetime, Marilyn's surprisingly versatile voice can now be enjoyed on quality recordings.

The best of the Marilyn books offer fresh insights about her. Some of the others are brazenly exploitative.

Three decades after Marilyn's death, her estate enjoys annual earnings of more than one million dollars. An enormous proportion of this income comes from licensing fees paid by manufacturers who wish to use her image. Marilyn Merlot wine . . .

. . . and Marilyn Monroe cologne are two products that would probably have pleased the woman who inspired them.

Playwrights have made use of Marilyn's larger-than-life image in a wide array of works since 1955, when George Axelrod parodied the world's most famous blonde in *Will Success Spoil Rock Hunter?* Some plays have utilized Marilyn as a symbol of exploitation, as in Tom Eyen's 1964 off-off-Broadway drama *The White Whore and the Bit Player*, while others have chronicled Marilyn's life as a tribute to her, as in the 1983 British musical *Marilyn!* Other playwrights evoke the myth surrounding Marilyn Monroe, commenting on its longevity and its cultural significance; notable works of this type include Patricia Michaels's *Marilyn: An American Fable* and Robert Patrick's *Kennedy's Children*.

A particularly heart-rending theatrical interpretation of Marilyn Monroe provides the focus of *After the Fall*, a drama by Arthur Miller detailing the turmoil of their union. Fans have assumed that the 1964 play contains personal references to the Miller-Monroe marriage, making for a gut-wrenching viewing experience. In 1986, Norman Mailer turned his preoccupation with Marilyn into a play entitled *Strawhead*, starring his daughter Kate Mailer. It ran for two weeks at the Actors Studio in New York, receiving mostly poor reviews. More popularized stage productions involving the figure of Marilyn Monroe include the Las Vegas-based revue *Legends in Concert*, which features convincing impersonations of Marilyn, Elvis Presley, Judy Garland, and other show-biz icons.

While stage incarnations of Marilyn tend to be used as metaphors or symbols, most representations of her on film and television amount to little more than two-dimensional impersonations used in superficial retellings of her life story. One of the most difficult tasks in interpreting Marilyn's life, particularly on film or television, has been the matter of appropriate casting. The actress playing Marilyn must capture all of the legend's signature gestures and poses without resorting to caricature. At least 30 stage and film actresses have attempted to recall or recreate Marilyn's charismatic persona—most have failed. Some of the more embarrassing theatrical-film attempts include Misty Rowe's vapid performance in Larry Buchanan's *Goodbye, Norma Jeane*, and Paula Lane's go-round in Buchanan's conspiracy-oriented *Goodnight, Sweet Marilyn*.

Television biopics run the gamut of quality. *The Sex Symbol* starred Connie Stevens as a fictionalized Marilyn Monroe. Badly miscast, Stevens could do no better than to exaggerate Marilyn's gestures and voice to the point of parody. Based on Alvah Bessie's 1966 novel *The Symbol*, this tasteless drama first aired in 1974. With its lack of sympathy and respect for its title character, *The Sex Symbol* merely exploited Marilyn; prints that played in theaters in Europe exploited the Marilyn myth further with nude scenes that were not aired on American TV.

Catherine Hicks's performance in the 1980 made-for-television biography *Marilyn: The Untold Story* is generally regarded as the best biographical portrayal of Marilyn Monroe. Produced by Lawrence Schiller, the photographer who took the famous nude photos of Marilyn on the set of *Something's Got to Give*, *Marilyn: The Untold Story* was based on Norman Mailer's "novel biography." The film was enhanced by the participation of three talented directors, including Hollywood veteran Jack Arnold. The impressive roster of behind-the-scenes personnel ensured pleasant entertainment, but the three-hour drama lacks insight into Marilyn's personality and fails to add anything new to the Monroe lore and literature. Hicks, whose thoughtful performance is the highlight of the production, managed to capture Marilyn's voice and mannerisms and suggest her alluring presence without resorting to caricature. Hicks received a well-earned Emmy nomination. (In an ironic twist, Monroe "replacement" Sheree North appears in this film in the role of Marilyn's mother.)

Nicolas Roeg's film version of the Terry Johnson stage play Insignificance is provocative, cerebral entertainment. Actress Theresa Russell—playing an unnamed character obviously modeled on Marilyn—effectively conveyed the combination of sensuousness and vulnerability that makes Marilyn so fascinating. Tony Curtis, Marilyn's costar in Some Like It Hot, played opposite Russell.

Many film and TV actresses have portrayed Marilyn; few have been as credible as Catherine Hicks.

A more thoughtful and intriguing depiction of Marilyn Monroe is found in director Nicolas Roeg's *Insignificance*, a provocative film version of a British stage play by Terry Johnson. Released in 1985, the movie is not really about Marilyn, but rather is a speculation on fame and the threat of nuclear war. The narrative revolves around the hotel-room liaisons of a group of unnamed characters—a movie star, a ballplayer, a scientist, and a Red-baiting senator—who bear striking resemblances to Marilyn Monroe, Joe DiMaggio, Albert Einstein, and Senator Joseph McCarthy. Theresa Russell, costumed in a white dress very much like the one worn by Marilyn in the subway-grate scene of *The Seven Year Itch*, portrays the movie star. Though Russell does not physically look like Marilyn, she successfully evokes her presence and image.

Other portrayals of various Marilyn-like characters include Kim Stanley in the title role of the 1958 drama *The Goddess*, Faye Dunaway as Maggie in the 1974 television adaptation of *After the Fall*, and Linda Kerridge as a Marilyn look-alike in the 1980 thriller *Fade to Black*. In each of these films, the Marilyn figure was used to symbolize themes and ideas that were larger than the events of the plot.

Marilyn has fascinated fine artists for many years. This striking, 40-inch clay sculpture by Canadian artist Christopher Rees was completed in 1989, and evokes much of the star's special charm.

Sculptors of another variety altogether dedicate themselves to turning out blatantly commercial items such as this mug and salt & pepper set.

The enormous popularity of Marilyn Monroe and her widespread identification as a sex symbol has led to the appropriation of her image by fine artists. Often, their intention is to use her image and to comment on its power as they evoke ideas regarding sexuality, commercialism, and exploitation in our society. Marilyn's career corresponded to an era in American art when painters began to explore the potential of popular imagery for expression. This exploration would culminate in the pop-art movement of the late 1950s and early 1960s. Pop artists were inspired by the ability of the mass media and advertising to generate images and emblems that quickly settle into our culture as commonly shared experiences. They were fascinated with the manner in which popular images could immediately suggest a product or communicate an idea. Some of these artists, including Andy Warhol, Robert Rauschenberg, and Claes Oldenburg, took familiar popular images out of their original contexts and transformed them into fine art, elevating them to the level of abstract ideas. In effect, the artists blurred the line between popular culture and fine art. Marilyn Monroe, with her emblematic quivering lips and trademark white-blonde hair, became the high priestess of pop art—often celebrated as a symbol of female sexuality but sometimes used to condemn society's commercialization of sex.

Early examples of her image in fine art include a 1954 painting by abstract expressionist Willem de Kooning. Though not a pop artist per se, de Kooning depicts Marilyn in his characteristic painterly style. Broad brushstrokes of raw paint create a thick texture from which Marilyn's image is suggested, only to collapse again into the chaos that momentarily gives her form. In de Kooning's painting, Marilyn Monroe has been reduced to her most recognizable features—a black beauty mark and a broad, red mouth.

A detail from Andy Warhol's "The Six Marilyns," a work that became emblematic of the pop-art movement of the 1960s.

Perhaps her first appearance in a pop-art context was in "This Is Tomorrow," a famous 1956 exhibition at London's Whitechapel Gallery. A photo of Marilyn from the *The Seven Year Itch*, with her skirt blowing high above her hips, was integrated into a work by Richard Hamilton that involved popular imagery from that era. That Marilyn's popularity reached worldwide proportion is indicated by her presence in European art as well, including a 1964 pop-art collage by Mimmo Rotella called "Marilyn Decollage." A large photo of a bare-shouldered Marilyn occupies the center of the piece. The photo is strategically ripped at her cleavage, underscoring the play on words between "collage" and "décolletage."

The most memorable use of Marilyn's image in fine art is in Andy Warhol's silk-screened paintings, which offer a disturbing commentary on the commercialization of Marilyn Monroe. Warhol first used Marilyn's image in 1962 for a silk-screen-on-canvas entitled "The Six Marilyns," or "Marilyn Six-Pack." He chose a promotional photograph of the actress from the film *Niagara*, blew up her face to tremendous proportions, and silk-screened the image onto a canvas six times. He manipulated the image slightly by using garish greens and magentas for the eyes and lips and by placing the color slightly off-register. Marilyn's fame rested on her face, especially her red, luscious lips. During her life, she worked hard to accentuate her lips, using a blend of three shades of lipstick plus a secret mixture of petroleum jelly and wax. Warhol's painting purposefully distorts her face and lips, emphasizing the artificiality of her image, and implying that it was a crass commercialization of that image that led to Marilyn's downfall.

Warhol recycled his portrait of Marilyn in a number of silk-screens-on-canvas throughout the 1960s, occasionally using it as wallpaper in installation pieces. He often changed the colors on the mouth and eyes, but always used the same photograph. No matter which of the versions of the piece is looked at, it remains the ultimate expression of Warhol's interest in the nature of fame and celebrity.

The use of Marilyn's image in fine art reached its high point during the beginning of pop art's decline in the late 1960s. In an acknowledgement of her identity as the high priestess of pop art, the Sidney Janis Gallery in Manhattan curated a 1967 exhibition entitled "Homage to Marilyn," which included Marilyn-inspired works by de Kooning, Warhol, Oldenburg, George Segal, and Salvador Dali. Culturally speaking, then, Marilyn is as much a figure of the 1960s as of the 1950s.

If fine artists have sometimes utilized Marilyn's movie-star image to represent an abstract idea, then popular art embraces her image to celebrate the woman. Three decades after her death, Marilyn's face and figure adorn a wide array of items—from greeting cards to playing cards, from ceramic figurines to bedsheets. Appealing to a more fan-oriented crowd, a figure of Marilyn graces Madame Tussaud's Wax Museum in London. The wax figure, created in the late 1950s, has been periodically updated to reflect changes in Marilyn's public persona. In a less commemorative fashion, her image continues to be used to move merchandise and promote products in commercial advertisements, including print ads, billboards, and television commercials.

Figurines are a familiar element of the Marilyn Monroe-merchandise phenomenon.

Thanks to the Marilyn Monroe bag, happy consumers can bring their favorite star along with them on shopping expeditions.

The art, the products, the books, the films, the rumors, the commemorations—all of these—are reflections of Marilyn's unique longevity. Despite the fact that her life, career, and problems are deeply rooted in the 1950s, she continues to delight us with her talent and astonish us with her beauty. In the hearts of many, she remains unsurpassed. Yet, her death casts a dark shadow over her image. We see that her innocence made her vulnerable, and that her personal tragedies carried her life to a sad and premature conclusion. The circumstances of her death continue to haunt us, for in death she has accomplished something she could not in life. We see her today as something more than just Marilyn Monroe the sex symbol. Her image has a duality to it now: Though she remains an icon of sexuality, that part of her image is undercut by the harshness of her life. Often used as a symbol of Hollywood, the image of Marilyn Monroe at once celebrates the town's glamour while reminding us of its pitfalls.

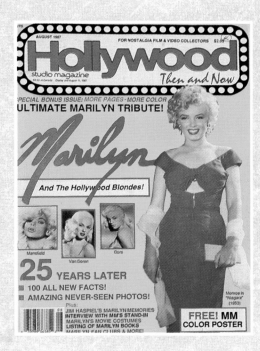
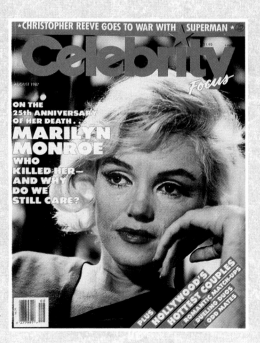

Marilyn's appeal to magazine editors—and to readers—is undiluted by time. Whether fannish or soberly analytical, the articles that have appeared with regularity since her death reflect her status as a permanent, valued part of our lives and culture. Far from being a ghostly relic of some dim past, Marilyn is very much alive.

The longevity of Marilyn's celebrity may result in part from the lessons she continues to teach us. In addition to the symbolic powers of her visual image, her life and career have been used to demonstrate any number of issues, from the hypocrisies of the film industry to the frequent victimization of women in a male-dominated society. Undeniably—and perhaps most important of all—her image and legend have the power to move us in ways that cannot be intellectualized. On a basic, visceral level, she is a remarkably powerful part of our lives and our culture. She belongs to us now—something Marilyn herself acknowledged in her unfinished autobiography. "I knew I belonged to the public and to the world," she wrote, "not because I was talented or even beautiful but because I had never belonged to anything or anyone else."

At the beginning of what would be a remarkable career,
Marilyn put on her best face for a screen test, circa 1946.

Note: dates given are years of release

SCUDDA HOO! SCUDDA HAY!

(1948) Twentieth Century-Fox 95 min. Color; D: F. Hugh Herbert. With June Haver, Lon McCallister, Walter Brennan. Marilyn Monroe as "Betty."

DANGEROUS YEARS

(1948) Twentieth Century-Fox 60 min. B/W; D: Arthur Pierson. With William Halop, Ann E. Todd, Jerome Cowan. Marilyn Monroe as "Eve."

LADIES OF THE CHORUS

(1949) Columbia 61 min. B/W; D: Phil Karlson. With Adele Jergens, Rand Brooks, Marilyn Monroe (as "Peggy Martin").

LOVE HAPPY

(1949) United Artists 91 min. B/W; D: David Miller. With the Marx Brothers, Ilona Massey, Vera-Ellen. Marilyn Monroe as "Grunion's client."

A TICKET TO TOMAHAWK

(1950) Twentieth Century-Fox 90 min. Color; D: Richard Sale. With Dan Dailey, Anne Baxter, Rory Calhoun. Marilyn Monroe as "Clara."

THE ASPHALT JUNGLE

(1950) Metro-Goldwyn-Mayer 112 min. B/W; D: John Huston. With Sterling Hayden, Sam Jaffe, Louis Calhern, Jean Hagen, Marilyn Monroe (as "Angela Phinlay").

RIGHT CROSS

(1950) Metro-Goldwyn-Mayer 90 min. B/W; D: John Sturges. With Dick Powell, June Allyson, Ricardo Montalban. Marilyn Monroe as "Dusky Ledoux."

THE FIREBALL

(1950) Twentieth Century-Fox 84 min. B/W; D: Tay Garnett. With Mickey Rooney, Pat O'Brien, Beverly Tyler. Marilyn Monroe as "Polly."

ALL ABOUT EVE

(1950) Twentieth Century-Fox 138 min. B/W; D: Joseph L. Mankiewicz. With Bette Davis, Anne Baxter, George Sanders. Marilyn Monroe as "Miss Caswell."

HOMETOWN STORY

(1951) Metro-Goldwyn-Mayer 61 min. B/W; D: Arthur Pierson. With Jeffrey Lynn, Donald Crisp, Marjorie Reynolds. Marilyn Monroe as "Miss Martin."

AS YOUNG AS YOU FEEL

(1951) Twentieth Century-Fox 77 min. B/W; D: Harmon Jones. With Monty Woolley, Thelma Ritter, David Wayne. Marilyn Monroe as "Harriet."

LOVE NEST

(1951) Twentieth Century-Fox 84 min. B/W; D: Joseph M. Newman. With June Haver, William Lundigan, Frank Fay, Marilyn Monroe (as "Roberta Stevens").

LET'S MAKE IT LEGAL

(1951) Twentieth Century-Fox 77 min. B/W; D: Richard Sale. With Claudette Colbert, Macdonald Carey, Zachary Scott. Marilyn Monroe as "Joyce."

CLASH BY NIGHT

(1952) RKO 105 min. B/W; D: Fritz Lang. With Barbara Stanwyck, Paul Douglas, Robert Ryan, Marilyn Monroe (as "Peggy").

WE'RE NOT MARRIED

(1952) Twentieth Century-Fox 85 min. B/W; D: Edmund Goulding. With Ginger Rogers, Fred Allen, Victor Moore, Marilyn Monroe (as "Annabel Norris").

O. HENRY'S FULL HOUSE

(1952) Twentieth Century-Fox 117 min. B/W; D: Henry Hathaway, Howard Hawks, Henry King, Henry Koster, Jean Negulesco. With Fred Allen, Anne Baxter, Charles Laughton, Marilyn Monroe (as "the streetwalker").

MONKEY BUSINESS

(1952) Twentieth Century-Fox 97 min. B/W; D: Howard Hawks. With Cary Grant, Ginger Rogers, Charles Coburn, Marilyn Monroe (as "Lois Laurel").

DON'T BOTHER TO KNOCK

(1952) Twentieth Century-Fox 72 min. B/W; D: Roy Ward Baker. With Richard Widmark, Marilyn Monroe (as "Nell"), Anne Bancroft.

NIAGARA

(1953) Twentieth Century-Fox 89 min. Color; D: Henry Hathaway. With Marilyn Monroe (as "Rose Loomis"), Joseph Cotten, Jean Peters.

GENTLEMEN PREFER BLONDES

(1953) Twentieth Century-Fox 91 min. Color; D: Howard Hawks. With Marilyn Monroe (as "Lorelei Lee"), Jane Russell, Charles Coburn.

HOW TO MARRY A MILLIONAIRE

(1953) Twentieth Century-Fox 95 min. Color; D: Jean Negulesco. With Marilyn Monroe (as "Pola Debevoise"), Betty Grable, Lauren Bacall.

RIVER OF NO RETURN

(1954) Twentieth Century-Fox 91 min. Color; D: Otto Preminger. With Marilyn Monroe (as "Kay Weston"), Robert Mitchum, Rory Calhoun.

THERE'S NO BUSINESS LIKE SHOW BUSINESS

(1954) Twentieth Century-Fox 117 min. Color; D: Walter Lang. With Ethel Merman, Dan Dailey, Donald O'Connor, Marilyn Monroe (as "Vicky").

THE SEVEN YEAR ITCH

(1955) Twentieth Century-Fox 105 min. Color; D: Billy Wilder. With Marilyn Monroe (as "The Girl"), Tom Ewell, Evelyn Keyes.

BUS STOP

(1956) Twentieth Century-Fox 96 min. Color; D: Joshua Logan. With Marilyn Monroe (as "Cherie"), Don Murray, Arthur O'Connell.

THE PRINCE AND THE SHOWGIRL

(1957) Warner Bros. 117 min. Color; D: Laurence Olivier. With Marilyn Monroe (as "Elsie Marina"), Laurence Olivier, Dame Sybil Thorndike.

SOME LIKE IT HOT

(1959) United Artists 119 min. B/W; D: Billy Wilder. With Marilyn Monroe (as "Sugar Kane"), Tony Curtis, Jack Lemmon.

LET'S MAKE LOVE

(1960) Twentieth Century-Fox 118 min. Color; D: George Cukor. With Marilyn Monroe (as "Amanda Dell"), Yves Montand, Tony Randall.

THE MISFITS

(1961) United Artists 124 min. B/W; D: John Huston. With Clark Gable, Marilyn Monroe (as "Roslyn Tabor"), Montgomery Clift.

SOMETHING'S GOT TO GIVE

(production suspended 1962) D: George Cukor. With Marilyn Monroe, Dean Martin, Cyd Charisse. (A few minutes of footage from this unfinished film appears in *Marilyn*, a compilation film released by Twentieth Century-Fox in 1963.)

●

Marilyn may have appeared as an extra in *The Shocking Miss Pilgrim* (1947), *You Were Meant for Me* (1948), and *Green Grass of Wyoming* (1948). Also, her photograph is seen in *Riders of the Whistling Pines* (1949), and her "Every Baby Needs a Da-Da-Daddy" number from *Ladies of the Chorus* appears in *Okinawa* (1952).

Irreplaceable Marilyn.